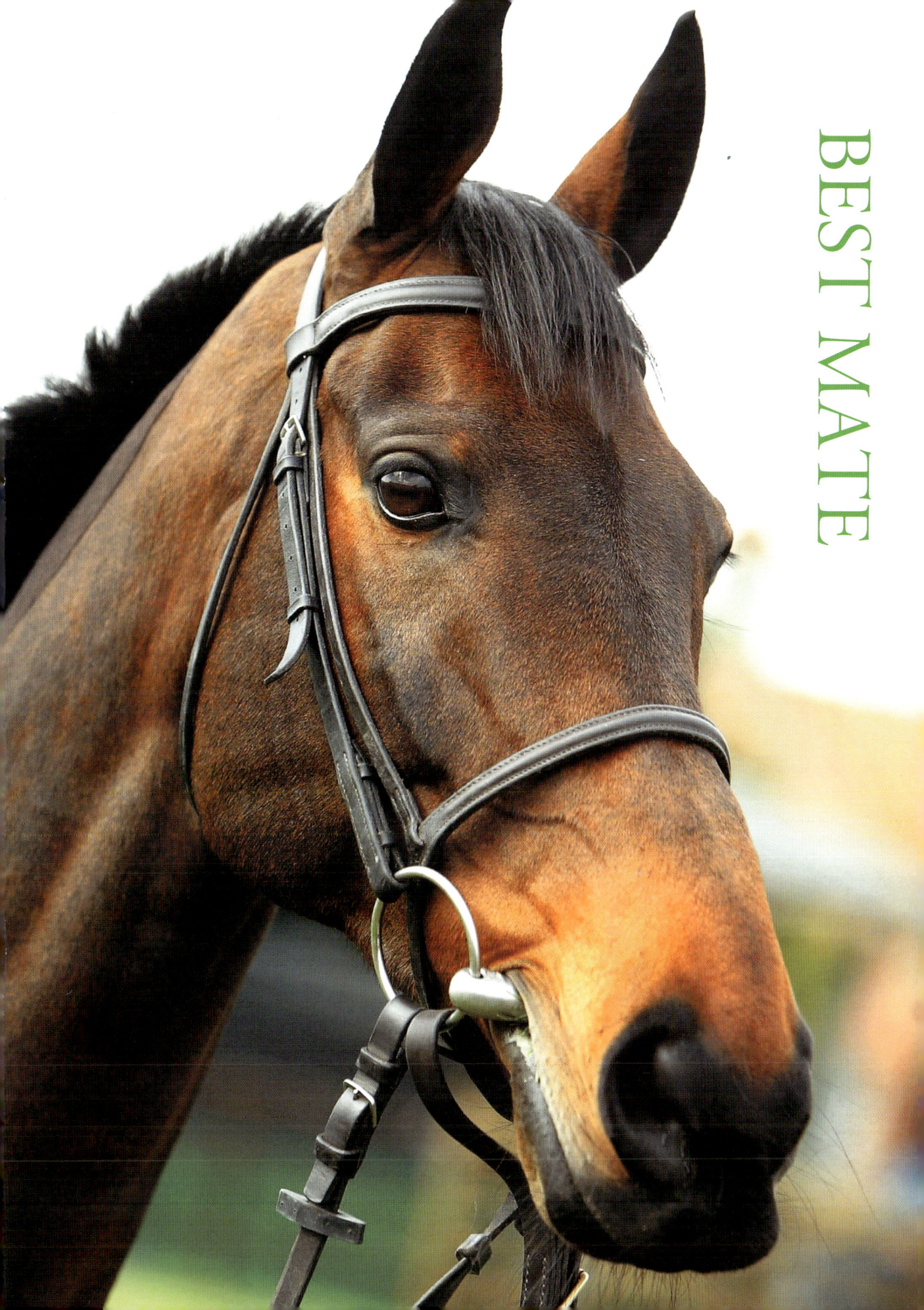

BEST MATE

BEST MATE

THE ILLUSTRATED STORY OF
THE NATION'S FAVOURITE HORSE

ANNE HOLLAND

ORION

First published in hardback in Great Britain
in 2004 by
ORION BOOKS
an imprint of the Orion Publishing Group Ltd
Orion House, 5 Upper St Martin's Lane,
London WC2H 9EA

A CIP catalogue record for this book is available
from the British Library.

ISBN: 0 75286 848 9

Designed by Harry Green
Printed in Italy

www.orionbooks.co.uk

CONTENTS

ACKNOWLEDGEMENTS

Out of the blue in spring 2004 I received a telephone call from the publishers asking me to write a book about Best Mate. Wonderful, no nicer subject… but then the challenge: they wanted it out in a few months.

Without the help of a great number of people it would have been an impossible task. Thanks to them, all the research and writing was a pleasure – and the manuscript, kindly and painstakingly proof-read by Richard Pitman, was delivered on time. Now I hope a wide readership will enjoy Best Mate's remarkable story, too.

I am truly indebted to all who assisted, so, in alphabetical order, my thanks go to:

Henry Beeby
  (Doncaster Bloodstock Sales)
Sean Bell
Gary Bivens (Weatherbys)
Alfred Buller (Scarvagh House Stud)
Owen Byrne (Jockey Club)
Harry Green
Robert Hall
Jane Hedley
Margaret Hedley
Natasha Houtcieff
The incomparable Jethro
Simon Kerrins (Tattersalls, Ireland)
Austin Lyons
Guillaume Macaire
Sean Macaonghusa (RTE Sport)

Damian McKeon (my computer guru)
Peter McNiele (Cheltenham Racecourse)
Ian Marshall (Orion)
Stan Mellor
Michael Moore
Alan Munnis
Philip Myerscough
John Oaksey
Racing Post (Brough Scott)
Richard Pitman
Liz Sanford
Terry Selby
Jacques Van't Hart
Rafe Warner
Declan Weld
Zoe

1

THE LITTLE BLACK BLOB

He was a tiny, wet, black blob, sprawled starkly on the snow, motionless. That was the only white about Best Mate on the day he was born beneath the shadows of mighty Trim Castle in Co. Meath, for more than eight centuries sentinel of an area more usually mantled in the forty shades of green that make the island of Ireland emerald. This is the place where the Meath foxhounds, the Tara Harriers and the Ward Union staghounds ply their trade – and where racehorses are bred and reared, some of them to go on to greater things.

An honest eye.

No one was thinking of greater things that January day in 1995, not even Jacques Van't Hart. Intuition had made him check round his mares earlier in the day than usual. Best Mate's mother, Katday, wasn't due to foal for another two weeks, but the signs had indicated otherwise.

'I could see something black in the snow, in the distance,' Jacques Van't Hart recalls. 'There was no movement but the mare was standing beside it, so I knew it was a foal – my first foal.'

A mare will normally seek the shelter of a hedge, away from the other horses, if foaling outside, but although the field had high hedges and a belt of beech trees, the first-time mother had foaled in the middle, exposing her offspring to the worst of the winter elements. Jacques Van't Hart hurried across three fields to where the foal lay.

'When I got there he was unable to stand. He was cold, shivering and obviously hungry, so I gathered him in my arms and carried him across the fields to the stable, his mother following and fussing about him. All I could think about was getting him warm and dry and fed, so I massaged him with straw.

'Eventually, he stood up on his own and I was able to put him to his mother to drink. Once I felt he was comfortable, I rang my vet, Ralph Warner, and Declan Weld from the stud where he had been conceived, and both said if he was standing and drinking he was OK.'

National Hunt mares are often mated with a spring foaling in mind and first foals quite often take longer than the expected eleven months gestation, so for Best Mate to be born on 28 January was exceptionally early for a future National Hunt horse. The little foal proved himself hardy but remained small. He was brown all over – no white star, no white socks and, far more importantly, no white flag of surrender. He was a battler, displaying the will to live that, in later years, would flower into the will to win.

Back in those crucial first few weeks of life, so much rain fell that even the Irish remarked on it. The mare and foal were kept in at night and fed but the little colt struggled to progress and lost much of his coat, possibly due to rain scald, making it hard for him to keep warm.

'He was doing OK, but I was worried about the loss of hair,' says Jacques, 'so I called Ralph Warner again.'

Speaking in the summer of 2004, Ralph Warner remembers, 'I had a good look at the hair loss because it was peculiar and I couldn't see a reason for it, but the foal was skipping about and perfectly healthy. I've checked in my daybook for nine years ago and I visited the stud on routine work for all the horses about thirteen times in those first few weeks. The foal was quite small but in good health and I never had a problem with him.'

When Jacques Van't Hart had to return to Holland to live, for business reasons, the mare and foal, then five weeks old, were sent to Declan Weld's Old Meadow Stud in Co. Kildare, where Katday was again mated with Un Desperado, the foal's sire. Declan Weld recalls the day Katday and her little foal arrived at his stud.

'With the benefit of hindsight, he had to be a champion. He was wild, like a gazelle, and tough, a little devil. We gave him extra milk in a bowl. At first he didn't know what it was, but he realised very quickly. Soon, when he saw the bowl arrive, he would come flying from a hundred yards away or more, but as soon as he'd finished he'd gallop back to his mother.'

Best Mate, the little colt, was a born survivor.

He was brown all over – no white star,

no white socks and, far more importantly,

no white flag of surrender. He was a battler,

displaying the will to live that, in later

years, would flower into the will to win.

2

TRIPLE
CHAMPION

A record number of 57,643 paying customers throng the walkways and lawns, the stands and the bars of Cheltenham racecourse, 12,000 of them in the new Courage enclosure with its Dawn Run and Desert Orchid stands. All badges have been sold out since early January. Bookmakers do a brisk trade and the Tote, newly rechristened totesport, achieves a record Festival turnover of £10 million. The keen sense of anticipation is almost tangible. Afterwards, people would be able to say, 'I was there.'

The sky is littered with helicopters, appearing like little black beetles to disgorge their occupants on the grass in the centre of the course. Some of them take off again, away over majestic Cleeve Hill

The crowds have always flocked to the Cheltenham National Hunt Festival, the world's premier jump racing event.

Arkle, victor of the Gold Cup in 1964, 1965 and 1966.

and the 650-acre bowl below encompassing Prestbury Park and the finest steeplechase course anywhere in the world. A light aircraft trails a banner exhorting people to part with their money on totesport, sponsor of steeplechasing's blue-riband event, the Cheltenham Gold Cup.

Out in the members' car park, luxurious hampers emerge from the boots of luxurious cars; glasses are filled, smoked salmon consumed, trilbies raised to acquaintances in greeting as they pass by, heading for the entrance turnstiles. In the stables, nervous grooms plait the manes of excited horses. It is totesport Gold Cup day, Thursday, 18 March 2004.

Best Mate has won the last two runnings of the Gold Cup. Not since Arkle forty years ago has any horse notched up a hat-trick, but Best Mate is odds-on to do so today. It will not be easy. A top-class cast is lined-up against him and as the tapes go up to rousing cheers from more than 60,000 voices, the dour French horse, First Gold, sets the pace at a fast gallop. All the way round the undulating first circuit, First Gold and his jockey Thierry Doumen set a cracking pace. Jim Culloty has Best Mate tucked in on the inside and the Irish hope, Beef or Salmon, is in his customary place near the back, with only Alexander Banquet behind him. Best Mate carries his head slightly to the left, an indication that he is still in third gear, but he doesn't appear to be pulling hard or fighting for his head. Therealbandit makes a mistake at the top of the hill and, coming downhill, First Gold maintains the relentless gallop.

Best Mate and Jim Culloty are led out ahead of the 2004 Gold Cup.

Another Irish horse, Harbour Pilot, third in 2003, keeps within reach of the leader as they head out on the second, daunting circuit, some thirty lengths separating first from last. Heading past the cheering stands, First Gold puts in a huge leap and Harbour Pilot follows him. Best Mate has moved up easily into third place, once or twice almost jumping into the heels of the horse ahead. Behind him, Irish Hussar is being niggled along. The field tightens up but still First Gold is jumping well and galloping away, keeping up the pressure on the opposition until, four fences from home, he doesn't rise so high. Best Mate is cruising effortlessly closer and to the thousands of spectators the contest looks over bar a fall.

This race is the ultimate test of speed, stamina, jumping power and the ability to cope with undulating terrain and Best Mate has shown he has all of these qualities in abundance . . .

This race is the ultimate test of speed, stamina, jumping power and the ability to cope with undulating terrain and Best Mate has shown he has all of these qualities in abundance, but there is another challenge to overcome – the cut-throat tactics of the opposition.

Here they are, virtually four in line, Best Mate poised to pounce on the inside. 'Here comes Best Mate...' the commentator hails, but

suddenly he has nowhere to go. He has been boxed in, more like in a big Flat or hurdle race field than near the end of a three-and-a-quarter mile chase. First Gold is still in front of him, Sir Rembrandt is to his outside and virtually knee-to-knee is Harbour Pilot, ridden by Irish ace Paul Carberry, and he is not moving out or saying, 'After you, sir.' This is no time for being polite and the commentator calls, '…and Best Mate is screaming for racing room.'

It is an immensely sticky few moments but Best Mate's jockey, Jim Culloty, to his eternal credit, keeps calm. As they draw near the second last, he sees daylight, pulls Best Mate across to the right, and then simply flies the fence, landing running. He is a length up going into the last, which he pops economically, but Harbour Pilot is sticking to him tenaciously and still the race is not over for coming fast up the wide outside is Sir Rembrandt.

'Harbour Pilot is coming at him hard,' calls the commentator, 'but Best Mate is all heart, he will not be denied. And Best Mate wins!'

Press cameramen dash up the track to the point beyond the stands

It was a tough one, but his resolution won through. Best Mate lifts his third Gold Cup the hard way.

where the horses pull up, recording history for posterity. Everywhere there is euphoria, and when the announcement is made, 'First, Best Mate,' a huge cheer goes up from the crowd, and they applaud him as he walks regally back by the stands and on to an ecstatic welcome in the winner's enclosure. Three times the victor of the Cheltenham Gold Cup – the little black blob had come a long way.

3

A LOT OF IT IS DOWN TO LUCK

Best Mate had been conceived ten years before his third Gold Cup triumph at Declan Weld's Old Meadow Stud, Donadea, Co. Kildare.

One of the most exciting evenings in Declan Weld's life, he says, was at dinner in Co. Meath with his French friend, the late Pierre-Charles Le Metayer, who told him about a French stallion by the name of Un Desperado. Declan particularly liked Un Desperado's sire, Top Ville, so he set off for France forthwith. It was August 1991.

For years, Declan and his wife Mary had kept high-class Flat-bred mares. For extra income, he would 'pinhook' foals from the autumn sales, i.e. with the intention of selling them on twelve months later at the yearling sales for a profit.

'But I lost a million,' he muses over a glass of good red wine in their lovely garden on a June afternoon, 'and the stallion fees for the Flat mares were huge.'

So, they reasoned, why not stand a stallion and reap the income from his fees for themselves? To buy a Flat stallion was out of their reach and thus it was they ventured down the National Hunt road. They acquired Satco, who produced Ireland's leading novice chaser Sackville, and Lashkari and were looking for a third when they heard about Un Desperado. Hence the trip to France.

It was not all plain sailing. Although Declan was mad about the

Jacques Van't Hart and his wife Deborah outside their home near Trim in Co. Meath, where Best Mate was born.

horse when he saw him – 'he was everything I wanted, I loved his head and his long ears and his whole demeanour' – the foals he was shown were, his word, awful. If they were indicative of the progeny Un Desperado sired, it wouldn't make commercial sense to buy him. Declan came home empty handed, but he couldn't get the vision of the stallion out of his head. Lying in bed at night, he reckoned, 'The foals can't all be bad,' and so he bought him.

'Yes, Declan is brilliant at picking horses,' says Mary.

When Un Desperado arrived, Declan's father, Wentworth Weld, known at the age of eighty for being a first-rate judge of a horse, leant on his stick, watched the horse come out of the lorry, and said to his son, 'You've got this one right.'

It did not take long for Dessie, as they nicknamed Un Desperado, to become a part of the family. He was a good guard, too – he would bang loudly on his stable door with a front hoof whenever anyone arrived.

'I had a passion for the horse and I loved him until the day he died,' Declan continues. 'When I lost him, I saw my life run away. We are a family here, we're not Coolmore.'

With the arrival of Un Desperado, Declan looked around for some suitable mares for him and his eye lighted on the French-bred Katday. She was the half-sister of two winning steeplechasers and had won three races on the Flat in France, but had failed to shine over hurdles when trained in Ireland. She had a curb on a hind leg (a curb is a bony growth that can affect performance) but Wentworth Weld came out with another classic remark – 'The hind legs don't matter, it's the front ones they fall on!'

Declan wanted to breed to a Mill Reef mare – Mill Reef was the great sire who won the Derby, King George VI and Queen Elizabeth Stakes, the Prix de l'Arc de Triomphe and seven other top races – but he couldn't afford to. Katday's sire, Miller's Mate, was by Mill Reef (as was the sire of Lashkari) so at least he would get the blood, if one generation removed. Declan was also moving with the times by looking for speed.

'Many traditional National Hunt owners, with the exception of Tom Costello, still like to buy the old type of horses who can slog through the mud,' Declan explains. 'But with improved drainage at most courses, and meetings abandoned when there is a lot of rain, horses seldom have to plough through mud like that any more.

'All Un Desperado's offspring hate the mud,' he adds.

Had Un Desperado lived, Declan reckons he could have asked any price for stallion fees after Best Mate's exploits, but he remains upbeat. He says of his current stallion, Quws, 'Yes, he's the next Un Desperado.'

Best Mate was one of just seven foals born to Un Desperado in 1995 because the stud had been in quarantine for much of the previous summer because of an equine virus, curtailing the mating season. All seven went on to win races. In Argentina, an earlier son of Un Desperado, Riton, held the world mile record. He was so popular that the crowds used to cheer as he burst out of the stalls and remained cheering all the way to the line. Riton's feats were reported in the British and Irish press and placed him on a par that year, 1995, with Cigar and Lammtarra, but Declan's phone failed to ring with impressed mare owners wanting to use his stallion. It took a while for breeders to latch on to Un Desperado as a sire. Then, just as he was getting full books, disaster struck. On 26 August 2000, Declan went out to the field to bring Dessie in to cover a mare and found him lying dead. He had had a massive brain haemorrhage.

'Best Mate will win a fourth Gold Cup, then I hope they'll retire him,' says Declan. He nurtures a dream that one day Best Mate might come home to live where both his parents, Un Desperado and Katday, had lived and where he spent some of his early life.

∾

The pharmaceutical industry first brought Jacques Van't Hart to Ireland and, like many another newcomer, he soon became enchanted by the country and its way of life, especially the horses. Longing to own a winner – which he eventually did, three, in fact – Jacques asked Declan Weld to find a suitable purchase, allowing him up to £5,000. Declan came up with a Busted filly called Zuhal for the sum of £3,000, and she never finished out of the first three in all her races. After a while, Jacques turned to breeding in a small way, which is where Katday, comes into the story.

In November 1993, Katday, owned by a partnership, was put in to Tattersalls breeding sales, and knocked down to Old Meadow Stud for 1500 guineas. Declan Weld had bought her for Austin Lyons of Summerhill, Co. Meath, but shortly afterwards Lyons changed his mind.

'I decided to stick with Flat-race mares and asked Declan to see if he could pass her on to another client,' says Austin. 'It was my decision to turn down Best Mate's dam and I can live with it. I'm delighted for the people concerned. We all need good luck, and at least I've had a good bet on him for each of his Gold Cups.'

So it was that, on Declan Weld's advice, Jacques Van't Hart became the new owner of Katday. She had won three Flat races in France but her Irish hurdling form was moderate, and she had twice failed to breed, so she was not expensive. Eleven months later, Jacques Van't Hart became the breeder of Best Mate.

Jacques's role in the Best Mate story was all too short, but he harbours no ill feelings about what might have been. Talking in the summer of 2004 in his beautiful, modern Dutch-style home on the thirty acres near Trim, where he now lives permanently and where Best Mate was born, he says, 'It's no good looking back. A lot of it is down to luck, and there were no signs in the breeding that Best Mate would be so good. I had to return to work in Holland for a spell and so, as I'm only an amateur breeder, I had to sell up, all four mares. That's life. I've no regrets. It's water under the bridge.'

Best Mate was sold in Tattersalls November Sales to Tom Costello for a mere 2,500 Irish guineas and Katday, back in foal to Un Desperado, was sold three months later in Goffs Sales of February 1996 for 5,500 guineas to Philip Myerscough of Baroda Stud. She had been prepared for the sales at Stonebrook Stud, Co. Kildare, owned by the Martin-Smiths, where she was shod by blacksmith Sean Bell. A month later she gave birth to another colt, a full brother to Best Mate, who was to be named Inca Trail.

'We all need good luck, and at least I've had a good bet on him for each of his Gold Cups'.

Now semi-retired, Jacques is planning a garden centre and is quietly acquiring a few more brood mares for the well-kept, post-and-railed land.

'I like to have the company of a few horses around,' he says, 'but I've never paid much for them. The four that I sold all produced winners, including Best Mate, of course. I enjoy looking into the bloodlines and doing the homework. It's very interesting. I have a National Hunt mare at present and am looking for a Flat mare, but I'm not in any hurry. I'll try to find the right one at the right price. With stallions, too, it's easy to go the fashionable route but I prefer to try to spot future stallions, such as Lashkari and Un Desperado.' He is unlikely to breed another Best Mate, but he receives breeder's prizes from his wins.

After selling Best Mate as a foal, he did not hear of him again until the year 2000, when he was still living in Holland – 'A friend rang to say that Best Mate might be going to Cheltenham.'

In March 2004, Jacques and his Irish wife Deborah were among the thousands at Cheltenham to see the horse they bred lift his third Gold Cup.

'Yes,' admits Jacques, 'I did think back to the day I found him and carried him to the shelter of the stable in my arms.'

4

'ONLY A SMALL FARMER'

Tom Costello describes himself as 'only a small farmer' and then, when coaxed, admits to 'having a bit of an interest in horses.'

The reality is very different. He keeps anything upwards of 400 or so young horses at a time and, in racing circles, Tom Costello is a household name not only in Ireland but also in Britain. His is a numbers game. This is the permit trainer who trained the 1973 Irish Grand National victor Tartan Ace and since then many of his 'babes' have gone on to great things – he includes six Cheltenham Gold Cup winners among his successes: Midnight Court, The Thinker, Cool Ground, Cool Dawn, Imperial Call and Best Mate.

Born to the horse-dealing world, Tom Costello has a good eye for a foal and can foresee how one might develop into a racehorse, an elusive art in itself. He and his sons produce a string of fine youngsters from the pastures around Fenloe House, Newmarket-on-Fergus, Co. Clare, in the west of Ireland. These youngsters are likely to have good pedigrees but he will disregard pedigree if he simply likes the look of a horse, most of which are bought privately, the remainder being 'pin-hooked' as foals or yearlings at the sales. He buys sixty or seventy foals a year and many yearlings, adhering to the old adage, 'fools breed horses for wise men to buy' – in other words, a breeder has to take what he gets, a buyer can choose.

The young horses are turned loose on the home pastures for three

Best Mate won his second point-to-point and is seen here with his rider Tony Costello and Tom Costello Jr (right).

to four years where they are fed and cared for, but the main nurturing comes from the earth itself. It is not just the amount of land that is important for a young Thoroughbred but the quality of it, too. Ireland, the emerald isle, not only has the rainfall that makes plentiful green grass, but the earth contains many of the nutrients, the minerals, that are so essential for a growing horse. It is what has made Ireland world famous as a producer of racehorses, both for the Flat and for National Hunt.

The Flat horses, bred more precociously – and more expensively – are started as yearlings and run as two-year-olds. Theirs is a quicker return, a faster turnover. The future jumpers need time to grow and mature. This is where people such as Tom Costello come in. They have the land, the time and the patience to 'store' young horses, and turn them out in gangs on the green Irish acres to grow, frolic, sleep, eat, play and mature.

After the Tattersalls foal sales of November 1995, at which Best Mate was knocked down by auctioneer Todd Hunter to 'cash' – actually Tom Costello – for 2,500 guineas, he was transported in a batch of about twenty foals to Fenloe House. If asked to pick a future super champion from among them, it is doubtful whether many people, if any, would have chosen Best Mate because he was still very small. These Co. Clare acres were his home for over three years.

By the time the youngsters are three or four they are ready to be sold, either privately or through the sales ring. Usually they are 'untried but well handled', that is not ridden and tested in a gallop, but educated enough to have been lunged and long-reined.

Tom Costello's secret, says former jockey turned racing TV commentator/bloodstock agent Richard Pitman, is that he has an indoor arena 'the size of Wembley' in which he loose schools his youngsters.

'It is his *pièce de résistance*,' says Richard. 'The horses will pop over a pole down one side of the school, jumping fantastically. Then he will send them on down the other side of the school where there is a full-sized steeplechase fence. These horses are only three years old but they jump the fence like stags. No one could fail to buy a chaser after that.'

On the strength of this, they are snapped up by trainers on both sides of the Irish Sea to fulfil orders for their owners. In the main, these owners have neither the land nor the expertise to have turned out a youngster and waited patiently for it to grow. Even at the sales stage, some are impatient for a win, but it is still a waiting game. Very often the horse needs schooling and to be gradually fittened up before being taught to gallop and jump. Sometimes, the late maturer simply needs time. A number of trainers have the initial work done by a livery yard proprietor, whose weekly fee will be less than that of a licensed trainer. Even so, the owners are paying substantial regular bills throughout this time and their reward may be a horse that meets with an accident or illness, or else turns out to be just plain 'nbg' – no bloody good. The owners, or their trainers, will have noted pedigrees, studied form of dam and granddam and looked at conformation from every angle, yet still things can go wrong.

Not every store horse will go to the sales. Ideally, they need to be fairly forward to do so. Best Mate was small and unlikely to catch the eye at the sales, despite his walk showing him to be a natural athlete. So, along with other horses deemed unsuitable for the sales ring, he was taken to some point-to-points, where there are often races for four-year-olds.

If the sales are Ireland's premier shop window, the point-to-points come close behind. The owner of a nice young horse winning a point-to-point will find a trail of would-be purchasers literally following him from the winner's enclosure back to the horsebox – no stables at a point-to-point – trying to be first with the chequebook.

However, whether at the sales or via the point-to-point circuit, from the purchaser's point of view, it is often a case of simply think-ing, 'I like the horse.' In other words, breeding is not an exact science, and this is what keeps the 'storekeepers' and the auctioneers, the

However, whether at the sales or via the point-to-point

circuit, from the purchaser's point of view,

it is often a case of simply thinking, 'I like the horse.'

middlemen and agents – even the sport of racing itself – in business, and those with an eye for a horse, too.

Ireland is home to many such people, one of whom is Michael Moore, a 'spotter' based in Co. Cork between Fermoy and Middleton. He will find horses for trainers, prepare and take young ones to the sales and keep brood mares at livery, mostly for English owners. For him, the point-to-point field is a principal source of useful horses. He will study the pedigrees of the entries, particularly the races for four-year-olds, then go to watch them run. In 1998, he singled out a horse he liked and invited Henrietta Knight of West Lockinge over to watch. The horse, Lord Noelie, proved himself to be out of the top drawer when conditions were right, and he ran in the 2002 Cheltenham Gold Cup as part of Henrietta Knight's three-pronged attack on the race, won by Best Mate.

Lord Noelie had already won for her when, a year later, Henrietta Knight received another phone call from Michael Moore.

'There's a horse you must come and see,' he almost ordered her, 'a horse of Costello's called Best Mate. He has a beautiful pedigree.'

The meeting was the West Waterford Hunt point-to-point at Lismore, a lovely part of the world. Dawn Run was reared here. Her owner, Charmian Hill, used to hunt with the West Waterford.

Michael Moore takes it up again. 'Tom Costello wanted Henrietta to buy another horse, but it was Terry [Biddlecombe, Henrietta's husband] who picked Best Mate out in the paddock. He was a smashing horse to look at but anyone on that particular day would have been dreaming if they'd said he was going to be a Gold Cup winner, let alone a three-times winner.'

Best Mate was one of sixteen runners for the four-year-old maiden point-to-point. He pulled up in the wet ground and Tom Costello wouldn't sell him until he had won a race. So second-placed Bruthuinne, later awarded the race on the disqualification of the winner, was purchased for the West Lockinge team. Two others were entered but did not run that day – Be My Manager and Well Then Now Then, trained by Michael Hourigan.

There was not long to wait for Best Mate to win a point-to-point. Three weeks after his muddy debut he obliged in a two-runner race, beating the favourite, Well Then Now Then. Be My Manager won at the same meeting and both Be My Manager and Best Mate were purchased afterwards by owners of Henrietta's. Best Mate's new owner was Jim Lewis in whose hands he has remained ever since, his jockey sporting the now famous blue and maroon stripes, colours that have helped to keep the Aston Villa Football Club in the racing public's eyes as a result.

That was the start of a fairy story.

5

THE TEACHER
TURNED TRAINER

Henrietta Knight was one of those pony-mad girls who never outgrew the phase. She joined the ranks of professional trainers in 1989 with three decades of all-round experience behind her. An accomplished horsewoman, she had hunted from childhood with the local Old Berks Hunt and in 1973 finished twelfth at Badminton, the world's awesome premier three-day event. She was chairman of selectors for the British Olympic Eventing team who won a silver medal in the 1988 Seoul Olympics. A breeder of Connemara ponies, during the summer she is sought after as a judge at major county shows, and in Ireland.

Home is in the little south Oxfordshire village of West Lockinge, set in the chalklands of the Berkshire Downs a few miles east of the market town of Wantage, birthplace of Alfred the Great. West Lockinge nestles at the foot of the downs on the edge of the Vale of the White Horse, a small village built in mellow brick and mostly revolving around the Lockinge estate. Mature trees line both sides of the approach lane and form a natural tunnel, and in one of the immaculate post-and-railed fields are lines of schooling fences. There are baby ones over tyres ending with a wooden 'coop', a row of five medium-sized steeplechase fences and, further over, a few bigger ones, probably nearly full size. A sign warns motorists to beware of ducks crossing the road and another one asks passers-by

Henrietta Knight
at home in West
Lockinge with Best
Mate and Inca Trail.

not to feed the horses. Some of the stables open virtually on to the lane, which is a public right of way. Occasionally, off-roaders tear up and down, but not at the time of day when racehorses might be out on exercise. The gallops roll into the distance. A green double-decker bus is used as a grandstand to view the horses at work. It's hard to imagine that this quiet place is just a few miles – a gentle hack over the hill really – from Lambourn, the Valley of the Horse, with its hive of training stables.

Born in December 1946, the elder of two daughters, Henrietta grew up at Lockinge Manor, where life revolved around Shetland ponies and general tomboyishness. When she set up on her own, she moved just a few hundred yards to West Lockinge Farm.

After she had done her obligatory year as a debutante in London,

33

Henrietta trained as a schoolteacher and found a dream job in nearby St Mary's School, Wantage, teaching biology and history. But horses still beckoned and gradually she built up a livery yard, taking in ponies, hunters and assorted others, some for starting, others for schooling, mostly for their owners to ride at weekends around the lanes of West Lockinge and across the rolling old turf of the Berkshire Downs.

In 1974 she quit her safe teaching job – the year, coincidentally, that Terry Biddlecombe retired from race riding – and progressed to a less certain but ultimately highly successful way of life, training Thoroughbred horses for those wonderful country meetings run by volunteers for local hunts, which are a quintessential part of English rural life. She set up a point-to-point yard, turning out more than a hundred winners, and a number of hunter-chaser victors, too, between the years 1984 and 1989.

The Old Berks point-to-point at Lockinge is a popular Easter Monday venue, providing one of the best natural grandstands to be found anywhere in the country. A steep bank offers several thousand

Open day at West Lockinge: Henrietta Knight with Best Mate, Jim Culloty and lass Jackie Jenner.

Lord Vestey,
Henrietta Knight's
brother-in-law
and chairman of
Cheltenham
racecourse.

spectators a perfect view of the action, which they can enjoy, along with their picnics and ample liquid refreshment, in a convivial atmosphere. At the foot of the hill, bookmakers set up in a line, calling out the odds and gesticulating wildly with their tic-tac coded messages to each other. The horses parade around the fenced-off paddock and tents provide changing rooms and officials' space. The commentator has a perfect view from the top of the green double-decker bus.

Point-to-pointing in England is less of a shop window than in Ireland – the minimum age is five – and before she set up as a professional trainer, Henrietta spent much time in Ireland, looking at potential racehorses under the tutelage of a number of top trainers, dealers and riders. She was learning, learning, learning – and she loved it. Her thorough grounding in equestrian sport, and her willingness to learn, her horseman's eye and her feminine touch, played a vital role in training the horse that was to become the best steeplechaser in the land.

Although Henrietta thrived on the work, it had its downside, especially lonesome evenings. When Terry Biddlecombe came into her world in 1994 (they were married in 1995) life really took off for her. Photographs taken over the past decade show how she has blossomed, smiling, sparkling, at one with herself.

Henrietta has had the patience to build up the sort of yard that she wants, allowing her horses free time in a paddock and schooling them

Henrietta has had the patience to build up the sort of yard that she wants, allowing her horses free time in a paddock and schooling them with gymnastic dressage exercises as well as putting them through the serious work on the gallops.

with gymnastic dressage exercises as well as putting them through the serious work on the gallops. Fortunately, she has owners who appreciate her philosophy. She trained her first Festival winner for her brother-in-law Lord Vestey, chairman of Cheltenham racecourse and married to her sister, Celia. Karshi came in at 20–1 in the 1997 Stayer's Hurdle.

Her patience with young horses has paid off and reaped handsome dividends. It has also engendered universal acclaim and appreciation of her across the whole spectrum of the racing world, from fellow trainers to armchair punters and all those in between. From her select stable, where she goes for quality rather than quantity, she has won an array of racing awards and has deserved them all.

6

THE PEOPLE'S HERO

Terry Biddlecombe was of the old school of National Hunt riders for whom it was normal to live it up in the Adelphi Hotel, Liverpool, the night before the Grand National – and the night after, too, revelling along with Josh Gifford, Michael Scudamore, Dave Dick, Tim Brookshaw, Fred Winter, Stan Mellor and Bryan Marshall.

Somehow, memories linger of times that were more carefree than now, less serious and more fun. There was not the pressure of riding at two meetings in a day, nor year-round racing. The two-month summer break meant that the jump jockeys could, and did, go on holiday, finding the sun, golf clubs and whatever else took their fancy. Life would be tough enough when they returned to the fray, with hours spent in the sauna, wasting away those extra summer pounds, heavy falls resulting in broken bones and enforced time on the sidelines, not to mention disappointing rides – but always the thrill of a win compensated. To win the Cheltenham Gold Cup, along with the Grand National, was every jockey's dream.

Terry was among those who always had to waste in the sauna, but he was up for plenty of good times, too. Good-humoured banter and repartee were always part of his make-up and, coupled with his blond-bombshell good looks, cheery smiling face and irrepressible *joie de vivre*, it was easy to see why he became the people's favourite – especially as he kept churning out the winners, 908 times in all between 1958 and 1974. Starting out as an amateur, he rode his first winner, Brunella, at Wincanton in 1958. He was champion jockey in 1965, with his best tally of 117 winners, and again in 1966, and then tied in 1969, sharing the title with his brother-in-law, Bob Davies.

Born in Cheltenham's county of Gloucestershire, the racecourse inspired him, much as it had one of the greatest steeplechase riders of all times, George Stevens, one hundred years before. Terry and his brother, Tony, used to sneak in to the races for nothing by jumping over the fence in Mill Lane by Frenchie Nicholson's yard, and watch the races from beside the water jump. Frenchie Nicholson's was a great academy for producing talented jockeys, Flat and jump, not least Frenchie's son, David.

As a professional jockey, Terry was attached for nine years to one of the top stables, that of Fred and Mercy Rimell at Kinnersley, Worcestershire.

Cheltenham proved a fine stamping ground, venue of many of his finest wins. On his first ride in the Gold Cup, riding King's Nephew, he was bowling along with two horses in front of him, when, at the notorious, slightly downhill third last, he turned a somersault, something that has been the fate of others both before and since.

Terry Biddlecombe with his former boss, the late Fred Rimell.

Five years later he rode Woodland Venture in the 1967 Gold Cup. Terry had considerable faith in this horse. Woodland Venture had won a Cheltenham novice chase the previous year when Fred Rimell expected him to be 'out with the washing'. He could still be, in Terry's words, 'a bit ignorant at his fences' and was apt to 'walk through' one if

Terry Biddlecombe
on Woodland
Venture (right) clears
the last fence just
ahead of Stalbridge
Colonist and Stan
Mellor in the 1967
Gold Cup.

he got it wrong rather than put himself right as the Red Rums of this world would do. 'But if the jockey could sit on him, he rarely fell.'

Fall he did, though, at the second last fence in the 1966 King George VI Chase at Kempton Park, a race remembered for being Arkle's last.

'We were upsides Arkle at the time and on the bridle,' Terry recalls, 'but of course no one knew then that Arkle had smashed a bone in his foot.'

So it was on to Cheltenham in March and, with no Arkle in the eight-horse line-up, brave Mill House was favourite. He had won the Gold Cup as a six-year-old in 1963, lost to Arkle in the following two years and had not contested it in 1966. Many people were willing him to regain chasing's crown.

Woodland Venture was owned by Harry Collins, a West Country farmer, and Terry tells the story of how Harry sneaked off to Yeovil market to sell a cow without telling his wife, in order to raise enough cash to place on his horse.

Mill House and Woodland Venture matched strides for much of the race until Mill House uncharacteristically fell. Terry had 'half-lengthed' him, that is to say, encouraged his horse to be half a length ahead of his rival as he approached the fence, then kicked for a big leap. This often results in the horse behind trying to take off at the same time but finding the task just too much and paying the penalty.

'To this day, Terry and I argue over who would have won,' David Nicholson, the rider of Mill House, is reported as saying.

With Mill House gone, Terry had a clear lead until, approaching the last fence, he could hear a horse drawing ominously near and the grey head of Stalbridge Colonist appeared close by. Ridden by master tactician Stan Mellor, this was the last rival Terry wanted to see.

Stan Mellor was the first steeplechase jockey to ride a thousand winners and Terry's quote at the start of a book commemorating the feat says it all: 'Suddenly, hooves upside. It's the grey. Sod me, it would be, wouldn't it? It's Stan. It can't be, but it is. It's the hardest man to beat in England at a run-in. He punches and kicks. He really rides out the last ounce, punching and kicking and bouncing – we always used to call him "bounce". And now he is closing, closer and closer. The fear of God's in me now. He's up on me. Is he going away from me? Mellor's the one bloke you never ever need in a motoring finish.'

Terry, possessed of a powerful style and a determined will to win, was not to be denied. Woodland Venture stormed past the post in first place – and Farmer Collins was presumably able to buy a few more cows.

Terry's celebrations, champagne in the weighing room and drinks in the town, lasted well into the evening, which earned him black looks when he was late for dinner with the winning owner and trainer – and more black looks the next day when, as a result of his festivities, he had put on too much weight to take a booked ride at Lingfield. That was Terry.

John Oaksey records another story in his book *Mince Pie for Starters*, illustrating the camaraderie shared between jockeys. On the last day of the National Hunt season, he was battling for the amateur riders' title while Terry was doing likewise for the professional championship. Both positions were still undecided after the afternoon meeting at Stratford, and Terry offered John Oaksey a lift to the evening Market Rasen fixture in a helicopter. Terry's chance of the title evaporated there but John's was just alive and Terry offered him the ride on what would have been his mount, much to the consternation of the trainer, Mrs Barbara Lockhart-Smith. John Oaksey takes it up.

'I was not privy to the conversation by which Terry – then as now the most amiable and affable of persuaders – managed to get her to change her mind, but not for the first or last time his irresistible charm won the day.'

The upshot was that John won the race, and with it the amateur championship.

Cheltenham remained a favourite course for Terry, and he added two Mackeson Gold Cups to his CV, with Gay Trip in 1969 and 1971; he was also second in the Grand National on the same horse in 1972. Gay Trip had won that great race in 1970 when ridden by Pat Taaffe.

During his race-riding career, Terry sustained more than his fair share of injuries and, together with his increasing weight, they eventually began to take their toll, so much so that he decided 1973–74 would be his last season. He had several memorable rides for the Queen Mother during the year, winning three times on Game Spirit, four times on Isle of Man, and scoring a double for her on Tammuz and Isle of Man.

His last day riding was to be the final day of the Cheltenham Festival, 14 March, and for the Gold Cup he was aboard the aptly named Game Spirit. The crowds were rooting for a fairytale ending, for both the Queen Mother and for Terry. Fred Winter's Pendil, ridden by Richard Pitman, was odds-on favourite, but they were brought down at the third last 'when the horse was pulling my arms out' Richard recalls.

Alas, there was no fairytale ending. The race was won by the inspired Captain Christy and Game Spirit came third – good enough for Her Majesty to commission a special photograph of her with horse and jockey.

Terry Biddlecombe and Game Spirit, owned by the Queen Mother, seek an emotional farewell at the 1974 Cheltenham Festival.

Richard Pitman adds an amusing postscript to this race in his book, *Fit for a Queen*.

'There had been a telephonic threat reputedly from the IRA to shoot the horse [Pendil] if he looked like winning. When I recounted this fact in the changing room after the race, Biddlecombe released my own tension by putting the matter into perspective. "Jeez Pitters, I was beside you all the way. They might have missed and shot me instead." Then he roared off to ride in the next race.'

Terry Biddlecombe's very last ride was Amarind in the Cathcart Chase later the same day. Describing the 'people's hero' going out on to the course for the last time, Richard Pitman takes up the story again.

I will never forget the wall of noise that greeted his emergence. The Cheltenham public gave him a send-off that had never been heard of before nor since. You had to have been there to appreciate the volume of spontaneous cheering, which must have equalled the noise the Aintree crowd emitted when Devon Loch looked the assured winner of the 1956 Grand National.

Although holding every chance of a dream goodbye for most of the race, Terry's horse cried enough between the last two fences and my mount Soothsayer went on to win. British racing has always been the straightest in the world and not only would it have been totally wrong to let Terry win, he would not have wanted to go out on a winner as a result of charity. He'd proved himself and held his position at the top through ability.

Terry had a boyish charm that oozed from him so naturally that kings or paupers would enjoy his company. If that was not enough for one man, he could also inspire horses to give their best with or without much persuasion.

Having almost robbed me of an early career winner when weaving a web of total untruths at the stewards' enquiry at Hereford, he put his arm round my shoulder and said, 'It was worth a try don't you think? Hope there's no hard feelings but learn from today. Talk as good as the race you have just ridden!'

How could you have any animosity for such a tousle-haired character, and he received just the same admiration from his horses.

It can be hard to adjust to life out of the limelight for anyone retiring at the top of their particular tree, be it sport, film-acting or organisations in the public domain. Terry had the surprise of appearing on the BBC's long-running 'This Is Your Life' pro-gramme in April 1974, but thereafter he seemed to fade from the picture.

He tried his hand at tipping and at training point-to-pointers, and he was responsible for the early tutelage of one of today's leading trainers, Nigel Twiston-Davies, but he was no longer in the spotlight, no longer a racing idol. He sought solace in the bottle, lost his mar-riage, attempted a new life in Australia where the bottle loomed large, lost another marriage and returned to England.

At that point, a friend, Terry Court, offered him a job at Malvern Bloodstock Sales – old friends had always continued to rally round him – and while working there he met Henrietta Knight, who had been invited to judge the entries prior to sale.

That they are friends is apparent

for all to see and together they have formed a key

partnership in every sense of the word.

Terry had been an idol of Henrietta's when she was in her teens. He began visiting her at Lockinge and she found he was able to give her not only sound advice, especially in relation to riding instructions for jockeys, but the company she so missed, too. That they are friends is apparent for all to see and together they have formed a key partner-ship in every sense of the word. People often remark on them being from different worlds but Terry is a good mixer and, just as an exam-ple, while Henrietta was a personal friend of the Queen Mother, Terry, through riding for her, was also regarded as a friend.

The banter between them makes their company fun, and the mutual support makes this one of the most endearing of modern-day racing romances.

7

LIVING A DREAM

Terry's arrival at Lockinge coincided with the arrival of some equine star performers, including Edredon Bleu. Some first-class owners were already clients, such as Lord Cadogan, Lady Vestey (Henrietta's sister), Lord Vestey and Jim Lewis.

Much as Henrietta Knight had quit a safe, regular job as a school-teacher to try her hand at training, so Jim Lewis turned his back on a steady, fruitful career as managing director of a bed manufacturing company to set up his own business importing furniture and selling it to mail-order companies. It became so successful that the Birmingham born and bred Lewis was able to exceed his wildest childhood dreams by going into racehorse ownership.

One of the most endearing of modern-day racing romances.

As a lad, his sum involvement with racing lay in placing his father's bets with illegal bookmakers. He knew even then, though, that the National Hunt Festival was the pinnacle. In the 1960s, as a young man in his twenties, he would visit Cheltenham, 'have a couple of pints of Guinness and if we had enough money left to buy some fish and chips on the way home, it was considered a great day out. Never in my wildest dreams did I ever think I would own a racehorse.'

When he began, he had a few not very successful chasers, and then he gave his wife, Valerie, a horse called Pearl Prospect as a thirtieth wedding anniversary present. It cost 12,000 guineas and she 'went mad' at such an expensive purchase.

At about this time he contacted Henrietta Knight, having read an article in a magazine about her burgeoning stable, asking if she would train a few for him. By coincidence, Henrietta had once half-owned Pearl Prospect as a youngster and so she readily took on the gelding, winning two races with him.

Jim Lewis, the very lucky owner of Best Mate.

Jim Lewis also had horses with Simon Christian and it was from his yard that he tasted his first big success, at the Cheltenham Festival, no less, when Nakir won the 1994 Arkle, the year before Best Mate was born. Nakir had been found for Lewis by French agent Pierre-Charles Le Metayer, the very same man who had been responsible for finding Un Desperado for Declan Weld in Ireland.

Lewis and Le Metayer formed a firm friendship and their successes included Camitrov, who was third in the 1995 Arkle, Impek and Edredon Bleu, who would be considered the height of most owners' ambitions. To date, Edredon Bleu has won twenty-one races, the last six of them consecutive, leaving him unbeaten in the 2003–04 season, by the end of which he was a twelve-year-old.

This wonderful horse by Grand Tresor had won two of those races for a small permit holder in France before changing hands as a five-year-old. He went on to claim the Queen Mother Champion Chase at Cheltenham in 2000, when Tony McCoy was at his brilliant best to beat Direct Route by a head. In the post-race interviews Terry Biddlecombe's humour was to the fore, as ever, when talking about the winning jockey: 'He's the most exceptional jockey. He's greedy to ride winners. He's quite brilliant. I reckon he's about a pound in front of me.'

Edredon Bleu won the Peterborough Chase at Huntingdon for four

The wonderful Edredon Bleu leads the way in the 2003 Cheltenham Festival.

consecutive years and in 2003, remarkably, a race in Clonmel, Ireland. Probably his greatest triumph that season was the King George VI Steeplechase at Kempton Park on Boxing Day, which he won at odds of 25–1, it having been decided to route Best Mate to Ireland instead.

Sadly, for Pierre-Charles, he did not live to see it. In December 2002 he lost his five-year battle with lymph cancer and died at the age of fifty-one. Jim Lewis was asked by the family to walk with them at his funeral, and his widow placed a framed picture of Edredon Bleu against the coffin.

Pierre-Charles had been able to see the success of 'his' horses for Jim Lewis, including the first of Best Mate's Gold Cups, and before he died he must have had more than an inkling about the future glory to come for Best Mate.

Jim and Valerie Lewis live at Callow End, a village of south Worcestershire, just a few miles from the M5, making the drive to Cheltenham very easy. The village pub, the Old Bush, has come alive after each of Best Mate's wins as fans celebrate wholeheartedly.

To own a horse such as Edredon Bleu would be a dream for any owner, and for Best Mate to come along in tandem…

Jim Lewis is both appreciative and realistic about his success and his luck, and has several times been quoted as saying he is living in a dream but when that dream is over, it will be somebody else's turn. His enthusiasm and ebullience, and his sincere praise of the team behind his horses, does so much good for the sport.

8

'ONE OF THOSE SPECIAL MOMENTS IN LIFE'

The first time the general racing public ever heard of Best Mate was a small mention in the *Racing Post* in October 1999, tucked away among more than fifty other horses, when he was four years old. The article followed a stable tour. Edredon Bleu was the rising stable star, and a horse called Red Blazer was, Henrietta avowed, 'My favourite horse in the whole yard – he's in my dreams most nights.'

A chestnut by Bustino, Red Blazer had already won five races, a bumper and four hurdles, but another two years elapsed before he won again. Then between November 2001 and December 2002 he added four steeplechases to his tally.

A bumper is a National Hunt flat race open to four, five and six-year-olds that have never run in any race other than another National Hunt flat race. They were introduced to Britain in 1978, modelled roughly on the Irish version that has been in existence for many years.

In 1999, Red Blazer was an eight-year-old, one of only eight horses that were older than seven in the yard at the time. The vast majority of the inmates were unproven youngsters – a policy the rewards of which, as we now know, were reaped with interest. Not for West Lockinge the precocious horses off the Flat, ready to run immediately, but the more old-fashioned type, fresh from the verdant fields of Ireland, from Britain and, increasingly, from France. Typically, a big four-year-old would not run in a bumper for fear of messing it up.

The horse would have a couple of hurdle runs as a five-year-old but not until it was six would its career over fences really get under way.

On the *Racing Post* stable tour another horse was described as 'not her sort' because Henrietta considered it unlikely to make a three-mile chaser. How refreshing to think there are still a few yards with this sort of outlook. There was a time when three-mile chasers looked like being in short supply, for all the Cheltenham Gold Cup is run over an extended trip, because more and more precocious two-milers were being produced.

A number of other youngsters in the stable at this time had run, and mostly won, in Irish point-to-points but time was still the primary key to their future. Be My Manager, who had arrived from Tom Costello with Best Mate, had been top-rated four-year-old point-to-pointer in Ireland. Henrietta considered both 'outstanding young horses' and even more time was to be given to the 17-hands-high Be My Manager than to Best Mate, for whom a quiet season's hurdling was mapped out, 'but we won't do much this year'.

Be My Manager went on to win a hurdle the following January, and two chases the next season. He was sold at Doncaster's May Sales in 2003 for 54,000 guineas and won two more chases for his new owner, Brian Murfin, and trainer Martin Todhunter in Cumbria. The Grand National may be on his agenda.

Interestingly, Henrietta was one of a growing band of trainers who disliked English hurdles, believing they cause too many injuries and that they are bad for a future chaser's jumping style. Like others, she preferred the French-style hurdles, which are more like mini brush chase fences. English hurdles make a loud cracking noise when hit by horses' hooves, almost like pistol shots, which can be very unnerving for a young horse, although top rails are padded these days. Another problem is that if a hurdle is knocked forward, it can swing back into the path of a following horse, catch him unawares and trip him up. A few English courses have now adopted the French style.

Sunday, 14 November 1999 was the day Best Mate first set foot on an English racetrack, nearly five years after he first saw the light of day in that snowy Irish field. He had grown up in the intervening years and one of the big advantages he had was that no one had hurried him, and this continued to be the case, thanks to his owner and trainer. Appropriately, the venue was Cheltenham – the third day of Cheltenham's 'Murphy's Irish Craic' meeting, formerly the Mackeson, latterly the Thomas Pink, and now known as the Open, whoever the sponsor is. The meeting's popularity has grown so much that it is now a mini National Hunt Festival and it will keep to the overall name, regardless of how many times the main sponsor (currently Paddy Power) changes.

The title Open is a good one because, apart from anything else, the meeting effectively opens the winter National Hunt campaign, coming immediately after the close of the Flat turf season. Cheltenham's marketing manager Peter McNiele explains further: 'National Hunt races are open to anyone to enter. There are no restrictions. Amateur or professional can compete at the highest level.'

For those who find the crowds at the Cheltenham Festival in March too much, or who simply fail to buy tickets before the sold-out signs go up, the November meeting is an ideal alternative.

For those who find the crowds at the Cheltenham Festival in March too much, or who simply fail to buy tickets before the sold-out signs go up, the November meeting is an ideal alternative. Attendance has increased to 65,000 spread over the three days.

Since 1988, the opening Friday has been dubbed Countryside Day and the atmosphere is completely different from the other days. The country sports fraternity descend to watch up to ten packs of hounds parade, to do the Christmas shopping in the tented village, and to enjoy top-class racing.

Saturday is the main day. The Mackeson Gold Cup (now known as the Paddy Power Gold Cup) was one of the first major sponsored races. The first one, run in 1960, was won by the marvellous Tom

'One of those special moments in life' – Jane Hedley with Best Mate after his debut win at Cheltenham.

Dreaper-trained Irish horse Fortria, carrying 12 stone and ridden by Pat Taaffe. He won again two years later but only once has such a weight-carrying performance been repeated, in 1965 by Col. Bill Whitbread's scintillating two-mile chaser, Dunkirk, later killed at Kempton when matching strides with Arkle. Run over two and a half miles, the distance is, in 2005, to have a championship race of its own at the Cheltenham Festival.

The Sunday, first run in 1995, has the atmosphere of a family day out. In 1999, the last race of the meeting, Best Mate's English debut, was the NSPCC Racing to Help Children National Hunt Flat Race.

Those who had seen him in Ireland the previous February noticed he had grown significantly, taller as well as filling out. He presented a picture of the perfect equine athlete, tall, graceful, good looking with a lovely action, excellent conformation and a handsome head. He was, of course, still young and immature, the type of horse a bumper is designed for, to give it racecourse experience without the hurly-burly of jumps to negotiate.

Out of the ten runners, five, including Best Mate, had never seen a racecourse before. Four had already won a race, and one of them, Phal, had won two. Perhaps it is not surprising that Best Mate started at never-to-be-repeated odds of 10–1. Ridden by Henrietta Knight's stable jockey, Killarney-born Jim Culloty, he beat a horse called Hard to Start, another newcomer, by three-quarters of a length.

Afterwards, Henrietta Knight told the press, 'Best Mate's a bit special. Terry and I adored him when we saw him in a point-to-point in Ireland and we were determined to have him.'

It was the perfect start to Best Mate's professional racing career.

Jane Hedley from Scotland was the first 'lass' to look after Best Mate. In one of those chance circumstances reminiscent of Arkle and Flyingbolt (where one lad got to look after two newcomers who turned out to be the best two horses in Tom Dreaper's yard), Jane, as a new girl, was entrusted with the care of the two new boys from Ireland, Best Mate and Be My Manager. An agricultural graduate from Edinburgh, Jane was on a 'year out' with a placement at Henrietta Knight's to be followed by six months of her own point-to-pointing.

Her time at West Lockinge was, she says, 'a life-changing experience'. She tells the story: 'These two horses arrived with a lot of fuss and "you must come and see these horses". It was my first proper job in racing [although Jane had already ridden two point-to-point winners in the north]. They [Henrietta and Terry] knew Best Mate was special from Day One, but they thought as much of Be My Manager at the same time, and a few people voted for Manager, he had the extravagant stride and the flamboyant jumping but not the brains, whereas Matey was a complete professional from the start.

'Going out for a hack he would act the goat and jump about, but when working or jumping he was perfect; he never put a foot wrong. There were about 20 of us, lads and lasses, working there; I was there on a six-month placement and had point-to-point and eventing experience, though not racing.

'It was a great thrill; for about a year after I'd left I used to cry every time Best Mate ran and think to myself, "Why did I leave?" Best Mate was a lovely-natured horse, but very much his own person – he wasn't particularly a people person, he liked to keep himself to himself, but there wasn't a bad bone in his body.

'His only annoying habit was when he was tied up to the ring on the wall; he used to swing his body over to block the stable door when I was mucking out so that I would have to shove him over ten times, but he never bit or kicked.

Best Mate at four, being ridden out by Jane Hedley with the string at West Lockinge. Even before he ran he was considered 'an outstanding young horse.'

'When riding him on the boring stuff, he would be cheeky and could put in huge bucks yet I never felt he was going to get me off. Once I thought "I'm going this time" as I was in mid-air, but then he got himself back under me for me to land in the saddle. But he was a real professional in serious work.

'With Henrietta's eventing background, everything in the yard was always just so; every horse had its own exercise, they usually went out in twos and threes; once or twice a week they would school on the flat. Best Mate thought it was a stupid thing to do, he didn't really need it because he carries himself properly all the time. Yogi Breisner used to come once a fortnight to pop horses over poles; Matey didn't do that a lot because he had jumped in Ireland.

'I jumped him in the loose school, but couldn't get with him because he was on springs, so electric, but Henrietta helped me and once I got the hang of it, it was a dream. I had tears running down my face, and they [Henrietta and Terry] got very excited that day, too. The great thing about Henrietta was she was schooling people as well as horses.

'I learnt a hell of a lot from her, and for the sort of person who wants to learn, she gives them every chance. I couldn't speak too highly of them; Terry was better with the girls, he was tough but would laugh and his heart was in the right place, but he had his own way of putting things.'

One of the most memorable days in Jane's life was Best Mate's first run, when she led him up for the bumper at Cheltenham.

'There was still a great deal of speculation about which one [Best Mate or Be My Manager] was the better. I mostly rode Best Mate, but I didn't say a lot about him, and when the day came he started at odds of 10-1. I didn't back him, I'd much rather just see him win.

'As I walked him round the paddock before the race, I heard so many people say what a lovely horse. He had such presence, then he ran, and he won, and everyone was beaming, absolutely delighted. When I led him back into the winner's enclosure, it was getting dark, and it was a lovely atmosphere. Then I took him back to the stables and washed him down, just him and me, and by then it was almost completely dark; he stood looking up at something and I thought "this is amazing". It was one of those special moments in life. He was a dream to handle. At the time I didn't realise just how special he was.'

After her memorable and educative spell at Henrietta's, followed by her point-to-point season, Jane Hedley spent three happy years working in Newmarket mostly on a Flat racing stud and then, in the autumn of 2004, took up the post of assistant trainer to Richard Guest in Northumberland. The lure of racing has drawn this talented young lady back into its folds.

When Jane left, the lucky lady to take over the care, and most of the riding, of Best Mate was Jackie Jenner, and she has been his devoted lass ever since.

9

'HE IS ACTUALLY THE BEST STEEPLECHASER IN THE WORLD'

Killarney is world-renowned as the jewel in the Ring of Kerry's crown, the most visited tourist area of Ireland and said to be 'Ireland's most vibrant town'. It is far away from the breeding and racing centres around which most of the country's Thoroughbred industry revolves, even though the county has three racecourses.

Among Killarney's scenic lakes and horse-drawn traps, known as jaunting cars, the young Jim Culloty first began riding horses from the back garden of the family's home, crossing what is now the ring road around the town to reach better riding ground. The Culloty house overlooks Fitzgerald Stadium and so Gaelic football might have been his game, but it was to ponies that young Jim was attracted. His father, Donal, had a horse in training, but his main interest, Jim told *Irish Independent* journalist Vincent Hogan before the 2004 Gold Cup, was always in betting.

Although Jim says he doubted his ability and took his school examinations (roughly the equivalent of English A levels) in case he didn't make it as a jockey, his father remembers it differently. Talking on Radio Kerry, Donal Culloty recalled, 'Jim had a particularly good seat on a pony as a child so that my brother, Frank, remarked, "He's so bloody cocky I'd love to see him fall off." He didn't always have the sweetest temper as a little boy but once on a horse he always had a smile.'

That smile has become Jim Culloty's trademark, not only after enjoying the thrill of winning on Best Mate, but in private life, too. He is not averse to hard work although he confesses he found it tough getting up at 5 a.m. to muck out in the early days.

Michael Doyle, the now retired manager of Killarney racecourse, said, 'He's a very good horseman and a very good fellow. He was put on a horse in a local point-to-point as a young fella and told that the horse had not been schooled but he showed no fear. He's a great man to present a horse at his fences.'

Jim was born just before Christmas 1973, one of the large family of accountant Donal and his wife Maureen. Jim had the brains to follow

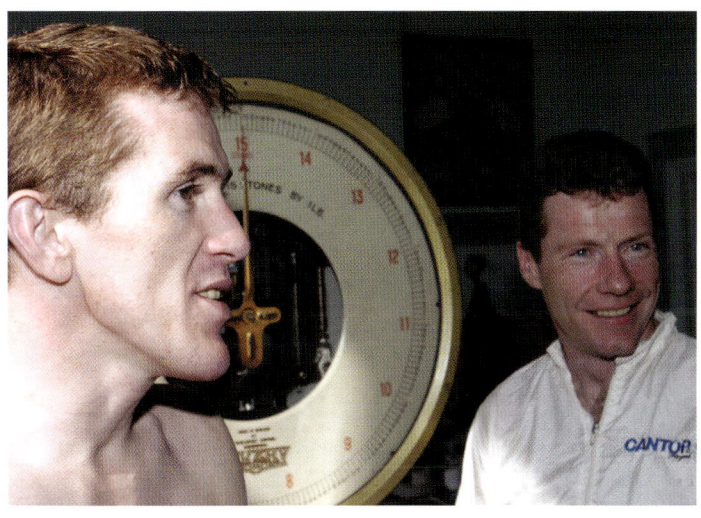

Tony McCoy and Mick Fitzgerald. Mick guided his compatriot Jim Culloty to Henrietta Knight's stable. The all-conquering champion rider Tony twice replaced Jim on Best Mate when Jim was sidelined from riding.

his father and two of his brothers into accountancy had he wanted, but he determined first to try his hand at race riding and, after riding in a few Irish point-to-points, he set off for England at the age of eighteen. There he worked with mixed success for a couple of point-to-point yards in the south west, riding a total of eighteen point-to-point winners between 1993 and 1995.

This hardly set the world alight, but his break came when compatriot Mick Fitzgerald, stable jockey to Nicky Henderson, pointed him in the direction of Henrietta Knight. Injury to Jason Titley put Jim in line for some rides for her and by the end of that first year, 1995–96, he was crowned amateur champion with a healthy forty wins. Three of these were in hunter-chases, including at Ascot and Huntingdon, two courses that were to feature in his life with Best Mate. The third was at Stratford-on-Avon where, on Proud Son, he won the prestigious *Horse and Hound* Cup for West Country owner/breeder/trainer Stewart Pike.

In the summer of 2004, Jim married his long-time girlfriend Susie

After his heroics in the Grand National the year before, in 2002 Jim Culloty went on to win the race on Bindaree.

Samworth, an accomplished amateur rider, and they live in Uffington, a village not far from Lockinge, in Oxfordshire's Vale of the White Horse. Uffington is one of several villages in the area to have a mighty white horse carved into the chalk hillside. With a post-racing future in mind, he has also bought a farm in Co. Cork.

Visiting his home course of Killarney during its Racing Festival in July 2004, and patiently shaking many hands, he looks around at the majestic mountains towering over the course and says, 'It's lovely here, isn't it?' The track has renamed its large drinking and dining area the

The track has renamed its large drinking and dining area the Jim Culloty bar – 'but they haven't bought me a drink!' he smiles as he shakes another hand thrust at him, then quietly slips out of the back door.

Jim Culloty bar – 'but they haven't bought me a drink!' he smiles as he shakes another hand thrust at him, then quietly slips out of the back door.

Apart from his own will to win, probably the biggest factor in Jim's favour at Lockinge was the tutelage he received from Terry Biddlecombe. Three times champion, Terry was able to hone and mould Jim's raw talent, and to help him mature, stopping him 'rushing his fences', and guiding him to becoming a horseman as well as a jockey. By the time Jamie Osborne, the stable jockey, retired to become a trainer, Jim was ready to fill his shoes.

Although Jim is best known as rider of Best Mate, probably his most heroic act on a racecourse came during the 2001 Grand National, when his horse fell and landed on the head of fellow fallen jockey, Warren Marston. With quick thinking, and regardless of his

own safety around galloping horses and flailing hooves, Jim grabbed hold of his colleague and pulled him clear. Warren's horse, incidentally, was none other than Amberleigh House, who was to win the race three years later for Red Rum's trainer Ginger McCain.

Jim Culloty has ridden Best Mate in all bar two of his races. He missed one through injury and the other through suspension. Ironically, both times the race missed was the prestigious Pertemps King George VI Gold Cup at Kempton Park on Boxing Day, second in importance for a level weights race to the Cheltenham Gold Cup. Under the Rules of Racing, a suspension begins on the eleventh day after a hearing, regardless of whether the days out coincide with one of the big races – and therefore a possible big pay-day for a jockey – or a lowly Monday meeting. The only exception is for suspensions of two days or less, when the rider is not forced to miss a Group 1 or Grade 1 race. Jim Culloty's suspension was for three days. This rule, understandably, leads to jockeys and connections sometimes lodging appeals in an effort to force a change in the dates of suspension when a big race is at stake.

With quick thinking, and regardless of his own safety around galloping horses and flailing hooves, Jim grabbed hold of his colleague and pulled him clear.

Under the rules, every rider has to try for the highest placing possible, but if he tries too hard, by hitting a horse more times than allowed with a whip, he will be liable to suspension for misuse of the whip. If he tries to 'nurse' a young horse, he can be booked for not trying, or for dropping his hands, that is easing up before the winning post. The general public must know that racing is clean, but judgement and common sense should be allowed to come in to it.

In Jim Culloty's case, his suspension was for dropping his hands in a bumper, the 'nursery school' for young novice horses, leading him to finish fourth instead of third on a horse called Beechwood at Doncaster, a four-year-old trained by Henrietta Knight having its second run.

Two years earlier, Jim was on record (in the *Racing Post*) as saying

Jim Culloty celebrates his Grand National win.

he resists the temptation to be severe on Henrietta's horses when anything other than winning is at stake. 'She wants the best for the horses and so do I,' he was reported as saying, 'and if that means ensuring that they're never abused that's fine… Our horses are all proper National Hunt types and are always well prepared. We spend a lot of time schooling, and I'll often spend four mornings each week popping them over the practice fences.'

Both times the spare ride in the King George was picked up by Tony McCoy, the all-conquering champion jockey considered by many to be the best of all time. Imagine the difficulty for the displaced jockey – longing for his horse to win, but dreading, as a result, losing the ride permanently. It must have been doubly hard for Jim because Tony McCoy already had the ride on the stable's leading star, Edredon Bleu, and that horse was in the same ownership as Best Mate. It is not unknown for an owner to insist that a champion jockey be given the ride on a top horse in preference to the stable jockey. To Jim Lewis's eternal credit, he did not 'jock off' Jim Culloty from Best Mate.

Jim says of the owner, 'He's an extremely sound man, an extremely good owner. He takes defeat as well as he takes winning, which is very important. That gives me great confidence because it means that if I go out and I think a horse isn't right, I can pull it up. We both believe there's another day with every horse. And that's the way Henrietta trains as well. There's always another day. They don't gamble. There's none of that carry on. A horse doesn't have to win today no matter whether it's right or not' – the philosophy of patience again.

He saves the best praise, though, for Best Mate. Speaking to Vincent Hogan before the 2004 Gold Cup he said, 'Very few horses manage to defend a Gold Cup but this fella's better than the rest. That's the difference. He's not just winning in his turn. He is actually the best steeplechaser in the world.'

10

'NOTHING FAZES HIM'

Three weeks after his bumper win Best Mate made his hurdling debut. He had already jumped round those couple of point-to-points in Ireland, and in addition Henrietta is meticulous in her schooling of horses, as she is in everything else. It is very unusual to see a horse of hers jump badly and Best Mate was no exception. Facing seven opponents in a hurdle race at Sandown, and starting as the 5–4 favourite, he beat Rosco, trained by Josh Gifford, by an impressive ten lengths, which prompted Henrietta to admit post race, 'I think he's probably very good. He's only a four-year-old and he might be something a bit special.'

At the same time, she earmarked perhaps half a dozen other young horses in her yard as highly promising although even then she predicted Be My Manager and Best Mate were 'two outstanding' prospects.

Best Mate, as we know, ran twice in point-to-points in Ireland, pulling up the first time in deep ground and beating his sole rival in the other. His presence, stride and jumping ability were what caught the attention of Henrietta Knight and Terry Biddlecombe and determined them to purchase him. Apart from that first educational run in Ireland, Best Mate has, to date, never finished out of the first two. His professional record, up to the 2004 Cheltenham Gold Cup, reads thirteen wins and six seconds.

Monsignor remained
unbeaten over hurdles
as he holds off
Best Mate (right)
at Sandown in
January 2000.

Two of those seconds came after his first two wins. The Tolworth Hurdle at Sandown is run over two miles one furlong and is often an indicator of future champion hurdlers. On soft ground, which he hates, Best Mate went down by two and a half lengths to the unbeaten hurdler Monsignor. After the race, Henrietta said she would not be afraid to take on that horse again, especially over a longer trip. She also said Best Mate would be entered for both novice hurdles at the Cheltenham Festival. He had run a cracking race in defeat, and she confirmed, 'I do think he's a very good horse, and he might just prefer slightly better ground.'

Best Mate's next run, at Cheltenham, proved controversial.

Tuesday, 14 March 2000 marked Best Mate's first appearance at the National Hunt Festival for the two mile one furlong Gerard Supreme

Novices Hurdle. Chasing was his intended future. Even so, Jim Culloty was bullish about his mount but during the race he suffered every jockey's nightmare – and was severely criticised by the racing public and press afterwards.

'Everything that could go wrong did,' he said later.

He had anticipated a good, strong gallop but what he got was a steady pace until the leaders turned on the taps down the hill, turning the contest into a sprint for home. Poor Best Mate was caught flat-footed. Worse, Jim, trying to make up ground hurriedly, steered wide round the outside of the horses in front of him, giving away many crucial lengths. He went down to Sausalito Bay, ridden by Paul Carberry, by a fast diminishing three-quarters of a length. With the benefit of that wonderful thing called hindsight, Jim admitted he should have waited until a gap opened up, as at least one opening most certainly would have appeared, being that far from the finish.

Later, Jim had to watch Tony McCoy produce one of the greatest rides of all time on Edredon Bleu, who was simply magnificent when landing the Queen Mother Two Mile Champion Chase. Tony McCoy lifted him to a short-head victory over Direct Route. The fact that McCoy was at his brilliant best and Jim Culloty was not cropped up

With the benefit of that wonderful thing called hindsight, Jim admitted he should have waited until a gap opened up, as at least one opening most certainly would have appeared, being that far from the finish.

in newspaper reports not only at the time but throughout the year, must have made it harder for Jim to bear. He admitted to feeling extremely low, but it was, he said, 'character building'.

He remained professional about it and, far more importantly, made no such mistake next time. In fact, that same meeting provided him with his first ever Festival winner – Lord Noelie in the Royal and Sun Alliance Novices Chase. He rode with intelligence and timed his run perfectly to master the highly rated Alexander Banquet, winner of the Festival Bumper twelve months before. Still it was for his losing ride that the unforgiving racing press and public remembered him.

Henrietta told the press she considered Best Mate a very exciting horse for the future. 'He's got a fantastic temperament,' she said, 'nothing fazes him.'

Henrietta told the press she considered Best Mate a very exciting horse for the future. 'He's got a fantastic temperament,' she said, 'nothing fazes him.'

This is a trait that is invaluable in a high-class Thoroughbred racehorse. An animal that gets over-excited and hyped up can, to use the jargon, 'leave his race at home' or, if sweating profusely, down at the start of the race, or the horse can lose by tearing away.

Best Mate had one more run that season, at Aintree's Grand National meeting in early April. Tremendous effort has been put into turning around the fortunes of the famous course since it was finally saved for racing in the late 1970s after years of brinkmanship and 'will it, won't it' be the last Grand National. Under the skilled hand of managing director Charles Barnett and with the backing of sponsors Martell, the whole place has been brushed up and revitalised, giving it a genuine festival flavour of its own, and with an excellent – and lucrative – cast of races supporting the big one.

Best Mate ran in the Martell Mersey Novices Hurdle over two and a half miles against four opponents. Notwithstanding his recent

Sausalito Bay beat Best Mate at Cheltenham on 14 March 2000. Here, Best Mate is in fourth as Sausalito Bay (right) jumps the last flight with Phardante Flyer and Rodock.

defeat, he was sent off at odds of 4–11 – reflecting just how much it was considered he should have won at Cheltenham – and as Best Mate put two and a half lengths between himself and the next horse, Copeland, the punters were proved right.

Afterwards, Henrietta confirmed that he would now go out in a field and run in novice chases the next season, adding that he was one of the best jumpers they had ever schooled at home. He had had five runs and to date that remains his busiest season.

Edredon Bleu goes head-to-head with Direct Route in March 2000 at the finish of the Queen Mother Champion Chase, eventually winning by a short head.

Next came his summer holiday, the time when, traditionally, National Hunt horses are turned out to grass for a bit of 'doctor green' to unwind, relax and grow fat and lazy after their winter exertions. They cannot be put out immediately, however, first having to be 'roughed off'. This entails gradually having their 'hard' feed of oats, barley, sugar beet and other goodies cut down, the number or thickness of rugs they wear at night reduced so that their bodies become hardened, and their shoes taken off. During this process the weather should be getting warmer and the grass growing so that the regime change is neither too

Henrietta Knight and the Queen Mother greet the winner of the Queen Mother Two Mile Champion Chase, Edredon Bleu.

tough nor too sudden. The sight of horses being turned out to grass never palls. They want to gallop, buck, frolic, roll and eat all at the same time, and it can be very amusing watching them.

When they come in again, the procedure is reversed and they are gradually re-introduced to training. Older horses usually come to hand quicker than young ones; they know the routine. The ones who have had just one season's experience, such as Best Mate, are likely to have finished their growing, filled out more, and generally matured. Now the world of steeplechasing loomed.

11

THE NEXT ARKLE?

Hurdling had been an hors d'oeuvres, a prep school, for Best Mate. He returned from his summer holiday blooming. Now it was time for the real thing. He had done enough to catch more than just the pundits' eyes. For once, many people did not feel it was an idle boast for connections to be cracking up their horse as a future star and so, naturally, there were many keen to witness his first run over fences.

The chosen venue was Exeter, a magnificent course two miles round, set high on Great Haldon hill in scenic Devon, and easily reached by driving to the end of the M5 and then on a few miles on the A38, a dual carriageway. The course's enterprising executive had arranged to put on a specially sanctioned race in November 2004, with Best Mate in mind, so that he wouldn't have to run in a handicap and attempt to give lumps of weight away.

Point-to-points, incidentally, are run at level weights, with the occasional penalty or allowance but no handicapping, making it quite possible for one horse to run up a string of successes.

Arkle, of course, often ran in handicaps, sometimes giving as much as 3 stone away and still winning, and he ran many more times every season, both facts being bones of contention between the Arkle versus Best Mate camps. Arkle had the distinction of having the handicapping rules altered to accommodate his presence; and he also caused the day of the Cheltenham Gold Cup to be changed to a Saturday for his third Gold Cup, so that more fans would be able to attend and watch him live.

That was a different generation, of course. Arkle may have been the best of all time, but Best Mate is the one today's race-goers want to see and cheer. Even before his first steeplechase, the bookmakers had him as a leading fancy for the Arkle Chase at the Cheltenham Festival, which is the leading race for novice chasers and often the pointer to future Gold Cup winners.

What is so lovely about Best Mate – and this is where he does bear

Arkle may have been the best of all time, but Best Mate is the one today's race-goers want to see and cheer.

comparison with Arkle – is his presence. He has that 'stand up and look at me', almost regal, way about him. With long ears pricked and head held straight, true and high, he is indeed the king.

The race was no pushover. Apart from having to jump fences in public and at racing pace for the first time, the opposition was classy. Two horses in particular were noteworthy, Bindaree and Shooting Light. By coincidence, Bindaree was to give Jim Culloty a winning spare ride in the 2002 Grand National just three weeks after his first Gold Cup triumph on Best Mate. Shooting Light went on to win the 2001 Murphy's Gold Cup.

On that race day in October 2000, however, they were still novices although they had both already run in a chase. Bindaree had won at Perth in Scotland, and Shooting Light had finished third in his first chase, on the Exeter course, a year previously. But come the moment, come the man. Best Mate's debut was almost faultless; he jumped beautifully and barely had to exert himself to see off his two main rivals comfortably.

'Just look at him,' Henrietta Knight was reported in the *Racing Post* as saying afterwards. 'He thinks he's Arkle, even if he isn't yet. He's a super horse, there's no other word for it. He's got class and he knows it, but he's sensible, too. Jim said he was brilliant and they couldn't go quick enough for him in the early stages. It's no good asking where he'll go next, but I think he could go any pace over any distance. He's got plenty of speed but he's already won over two and a half miles. He's very special. Probably the best we've had so far.'

'He thinks he's Arkle, even if he isn't yet. He's a super horse, there's no other word for it. He's got class and he knows it, but he's sensible, too.'

Those were prophetic words, the more so when you remember that Henrietta already had the reigning Queen Mother Champion Chaser, Edredon Bleu, in her care. Even at this early stage in Best Mate's career, Jim Culloty was nurturing Gold Cup dreams.

Two more easy wins furthered Best Mate's claims. At the popular November Open meeting at Cheltenham he made his first semblance of a mistake, at the ditch at the top of the hill, but he brushed it aside and went on to beat Fatehalkhair by eighteen lengths at odds of 8–13. It can help a Festival-bound novice horse to have experience of the course in advance, to learn its switchback ways and demanding fences. Dawn Run springs to mind; she unseated Tony Mullins at that same ditch at the top of the hill, but she learnt from it and returned two months later to win one of the most memorable of all Gold Cups.

After the win, Terry Biddlecombe commented that Best Mate 'was just getting complacent and dropped his hind legs in the ditch, but Jim gave him time to recover and get balanced starting down the hill again.'

Henrietta said, 'This horse really does think he's Arkle although that's a bit unfair on Arkle. He has a lovely temperament and such an air about him. If all goes well and he gets the luck, I think he can go right to the top – he's a true athlete. He will have one more run before the Arkle, but I'm not sure at this stage whether we will give him a break now or not, as he's so well at the moment. But I suspect we'll do the same as Edredon Bleu, in that we'll give him a rest and bring him back for a run six weeks before the Festival. He goes on any ground and any distance. It's the Arkle this year and the Gold Cup next year.'

So that was it, firmly stated. Best Mate was considered a future Gold Cup horse. Many spectators who were there that day agreed.

Best Mate had his break and it was nearly three months before he reappeared. As usual, his fitness was not in doubt and he looked magnificent. He was beginning to attract a following among the public, and those who watched his thirteen-length victory over two miles five furlongs at Sandown in February were left in no doubt about his ability. An outstanding display of chasing was described by one journalist, Bruce Jackson in the *Racing Post*, as a saunter. Jim Culloty found that Best Mate was not only athletic and agile but also, excitingly, had a whole range of gears and scintillating acceleration. What a dream horse to ride.

'He was foot perfect,' Jim declared post race. 'I couldn't have been more impressed with him. He's lived up to his name now.'

After the race, Terry Biddlecombe received a call from his long-time friend, former jockey Dave Dick, joking how much he would like to ride and win on Best Mate in the Gold Cup, saying he was the best horse he had seen in years. Two weeks later the seventy-six-year-old Dave Dick died. As a jockey, he won the Grand National on ESB after Devon Loch's collapse, the Gold Cup on Mont Tremblant, and he also won the Lincoln Handicap on the Flat.

Best Mate had now won all three of his steeplechases and connections openly talked about him as a Gold Cup horse. The attempt was not to be made for another year but his price was cut from 33–1 to 20–1. First, he was heading for the Arkle and, with the unbeaten hat-trick beneath his belt, he became a short-priced favourite.

However, fate intervened. There was to be no Arkle Chase. There was to be no Cheltenham Gold Cup. There would be no Cheltenham Festival in 2001 at all. Foot and mouth disease devastated the rural community throughout Britain, causing untold hardship and heart-

break, and although Cheltenham attempted to keep going, a confirmed case among sheep within the trigger zone just days before the event left the executive with no alternative but to cancel.

Peter McNiele sums up the situation succinctly. 'It was a tricky year, 2001, and hugely disappointing. The fact that the rules focused on red tape rather than animal welfare made it even worse. Every cloud has a silver lining, however, as the Open thrived on the back of it and progressed significantly that year.'

The racing world could only commiserate with their country cousins during the outbreak – and do whatever they could to find alternatives for their horses. For a long time it was touch and go whether or not the Aintree meeting would survive and even then, after it got the nod, the heavens opened and the fixture was jeopardised by the weather.

With no steeplechase considered suitable for Best Mate, he ran in a hurdle and, on the heavy ground, he was well beaten by Barton. Barton had won eight consecutive hurdle races in the previous two years until his two runs before this outing, so it is a tremendous compliment to Best Mate that chasing's new star should have started favourite. But whereas the specialist hurdler made light of the heavy ground, for Best Mate it was a dour trek through the mud.

Jim Lewis commented, 'Best Mate is a tough cookie. It's very testing out there, and Jim Culloty said the horse was going up to his knees in some places.'

Best Mate was retired for the season, unbeaten over fences, and it was announced that he would step up in trip the next season. The mantle of being 'the next Arkle' was resting lightly around Best Mate's shoulders.

With the 2001 Cheltenham Festival cancelled due to the foot and mouth outbreak, Best Mate was re-routed to Aintree for a run over hurdles, where Barton (pictured here, a year later) beat him.

The mantle of being 'the next Arkle' was resting lightly around Best Mate's shoulders.

12

TATTERSALLS

In June 2001, with Best Mate's second season safely behind him and a scoresheet of six wins and three seconds from as many runs, his two years younger full brother Cornish Rebel, that is with the same dam and sire, came up for sale at Tattersalls Derby Sale in Ireland.

Traditionally, this is Ireland's biggest National Hunt shop window. Purpose-built in the late 1980s at Fairyhouse, opposite the racetrack that hosts the Irish Grand National every Easter Monday, the huge complex in rural Co. Meath becomes a mecca for would-be buyers from England, America, France, Ireland and elsewhere every June.

The winners of numerous high-class National Hunt races on both sides of the Irish Sea have passed through its hands, including, by 2004, the winners of all seven Cheltenham Gold Cups from 1998, the last three of those being Best Mate, who was sold there as a foal. The others were Looks Like Trouble, See More Business, Cool Dawn and Mr Mulligan.

Grand National winners Amberleigh House, Monty's Pass and Bindaree have also passed through its ring, while the two-miler Moscow Flyer was sold for 17,000 guineas in 1998 to Jessica Harrington, who has a knowing eye for young horses. The lovely Rhinestone Cowboy is another graduate, having been sold for 82,000 guineas in 1999.

The November sales, at which Best Mate was sold, accommodate those recently weaned, as well as brood mares and some young stock.

picked Looks Like Trouble, who started favourite at 9–2. Best Mate was 7–1.

At the fall of the flag on the afternoon of 14 March 2002, Looks Like Trouble set off in front, aiming to keep his crown. Jim Culloty, finding himself in a sea of horses, switched Best Mate to the inside. Looks Like Trouble, ridden by Richard Johnson, was still in the lead coming down the hill for the last time when the strain began to tell and his jumping suffered. A group of four, led by See More Business, began to put daylight between them and him, but the twelve-year-old victor of 1999 could not shake off Best Mate, who was simply cruising

Commanche Court finished second in the 2002 Gold Cup, trained by Ted Walsh and ridden by his son, Ruby.

in Jim Culloty's hands. It was left to Irish horse Commanche Court to mount the main challenge but Best Mate sailed by imperiously as if he was fly swatting to record a one-and-three-quarter length victory. As he walked back in, he was barely blowing from his exertions.

Commanche Court was 25–1 and See More Business, taking third, was a virtually unconsidered 40–1. The gallant Marlborough filled fourth spot for trainer Nicky Henderson. Although he is one of

PREVIOUS PAGES
After jumping the second last fence, Best Mate (left) comes through on the inside to pass Commanche Court and See More Business.

The famous greeting…

Cheltenham's most successful trainers, this was his first runner in the race for twenty years, illustrating how difficult it is to make the Tote Gold Cup, even from a stable that has the greatest strength in depth. Thirteen finished and after the race Looks Like Trouble, who came in last, was retired. Of Henrietta's other two runners, Lord Noelie was tenth and Go Ballistic, who was running in the Gold Cup for the fifth time in his career, pulled up.

In the cheering that followed, television viewers saw the first of the now famous embraces between Henrietta Knight and Terry Biddle-combe, tearful, joyous, emotional. For Jim Culloty there was an embrace from his mother as he unsaddled, and from his girlfriend, now his wife, Susie Samworth.

Henrietta told the waiting press, 'I knew he'd win from two out. He is just poetry in motion and he is a dream to train, too. He does everything right, the perfect schoolboy. Jim gave him a super ride and he always had him in the right place.

'My only doubt,' she added, 'was that this race might have come a year too soon because it is only his second season chasing. I was worried we would be asking too much too soon, but he's answered every question to date.'

Jim Culloty said, 'I always knew I had enough horse under me to catch the leaders. You couldn't say he'd get the trip until he tried it, but he proved us right. This is unreal. This is the pinnacle. Where do you go from here?'

The answer to that came three weeks later when, on a spare ride picked up following injury to a fellow jockey, he won the Grand National on Bindaree. This was the stuff of fairytales.

The Cheltenham winner's enclosure was fairytale enough for Best Mate's ecstatic owner Jim Lewis, who treated the applauding crowds to a rendition of his horse's name sung to the tune of 'Amazing Grace'. For Jim Lewis, who as a boy would run to the bookie's for his dad, it was a dream come true. Sporting the colours of Aston Villa Football Club's 1957 FA Cup Final winning strip, he said, 'I came here thinking if he finished in the first four he'd come back with a better chance

next year. Henrietta is a weaver of dreams. She and I have been sharing the dream and we've never lost faith. This is my best horse by a million miles,' and that from the man who also owns the great Edredon Bleu and before he could know just how great Best Mate was to be.

Journalist Alastair Down has a potent pen, and his *Racing Post* piece next day included fulsome praise and apt comment. He wrote:

'Best Mate has long looked one of the classiest chasing recruits of recent years and he rammed home the extent of his potential with an emphatic victory in the Gold Cup…

This was a Gold Cup run at championship pace and in addition to producing a winner who is patently all class, it also featured two stirring performances from the placed horses…

Best Mate's triumph was a grass roots jumping result. Knight was not born short of life's little privileges, but she is splendidly down to earth and possessed of a very salty turn of phrase when she feels the occasion demands. A National Hunt woman to the core, she has at her side one of the legends of the game in Terry Biddlecombe.

… They have never wavered in their belief that Best Mate was exceptional and for my money the making of the horse was when he got his backside warmed in defeat at Ascot by Wahiba Sands and also when he had to get tough in the King George behind Florida Pearl. His sheer ability has often made him an easy winner, but Gold Cup winners need to know about the reality of battle and not be freaked by them. This season Best Mate has become a man and the seeds of his victory lay in those two defeats.

Immediate reaction was that at just seven years old, here we have a rising star with the potential to come back for more Gold Cups.'

The young pretender was crowned. Long live the young pretender.

A number of scribes noted that Best Mate had more to do before joining steeplechasing's élite, to which connections could understandably answer that, given time, that's exactly what they intended to do. It was made crystal clear, however, that he would not run again that season.

Speaking to the press during a sparkling reception at Lockinge, the day after his Gold Cup victory, Henrietta said they 'wouldn't dream of asking such a young horse to run again this season. He's the type to improve and strengthen up, so there's no point in rushing him.'

He would be aimed for a repeat at November's Haldon Gold Cup at Exeter. She said of the 'horse with no flaws' that 'he could win at Badminton, in the show ring and just about everywhere else – he'd be brilliant at dressage.'

LEFT Jim Culloty celebrates winning the Gold Cup in 2002.

RIGHT The happy owner, Jim Lewis, enjoys the moment with the Princess Royal.

Two days after Best Mate's Gold Cup win, a striking big brown five-year-old called Kingscliff won a lowly point-to-point at Larkhill. He was trained by Sally Alner, wife of National Hunt trainer and former leading amateur rider Robert. A few years before, former point-to-pointer Cool Dawn had swapped Sally's yard for Robert's next door and had gone on to win the 1998 Cheltenham Gold Cup. Other former point-to-pointers that have won the Gold Cup are See More Business (1999), The Dikler (1973) and the 100–1 Norton's Coin (1990).

The 'amateur route' provides a different type of education. Instead of hurdling, the horse goes hunting, and in the hunting field he learns to think for himself, get out of tricky situations, pick his feet up and jump different types of obstacles. A horse that goes hunting will never get bored or stale – and it has made many a jockey, too, notably Paul Carberry. Crossing the huge ditches in Co. Meath makes a horseman out of a jockey, one that will not be dislodged easily from the saddle.

Larkhill point-to-point course, an exceptionally long circuit of about two miles, suits an out-and-out galloper, and also has fairly stiff fences. It suited Kingscliff ideally and two years later, he was to be ante-post second favourite to Best Mate for the 2004 Gold Cup.

Best Mate, perhaps surprisingly, did not top the 2001–02 season's Anglo-Irish Jumps Classifications, published in May, that accolade going to the marvellous Florida Pearl. However, Best Mate was named National Hunt Horse of the Year in a poll of Racegoers' Club members, taking 44 per cent of the vote; and he topped the *Racing Post*'s list of top performers with a rating of 186, two points ahead of both Commanche Court and Florida Pearl. Henrietta Knight's Lord Noelie was in joint seventh with Tiutchev and Shooting Light while her stalwart Edredon Bleu was in joint ninth with Behrajan. Three in the top ten was no mean achievement but rather than rest on their laurels, she and Terry went shopping in Ireland again.

14

DONCASTER SALES

In May most National Hunt eyes are turned on the Doncaster Spring Sales. Held at the end of May – from Monday 27 to Friday 31 in 2002 – the Doncaster Bloodstock Sales are billed as the world's premier National Hunt sales. Two days for store horses – three-and four-year-olds that are not yet tried let alone raced – are followed by three days for horses in training and point-to-pointers. In 2002, exactly 1,000 lots were catalogued. The store horses included a half-brother to the newly crowned top steeplechaser, Best Mate, and as such was certain to be hot property.

Doncaster Bloodstock Sales were founded in the early 1960s by two racing friends, Ken Oliver from Scotland and Willie Stephenson from Royston, Hertfordshire. They each put £150 in to the venture; it now has an annual turnover of several million pounds. One of their early decisions was to acquire the services of a remarkable auctioneer, Harry Beeby, and, in later years, his son, Henry.

Ken Oliver and Willie Stephenson had a similar outlook on life – hard work and hard play in equal measures. As they gradually revamped and modernised the premises, situated in the stable yards of Doncaster Race-course, they ensured a capacious bar was built close to the selling ring, so that potential bidders would never be too far away! They also tapped in to the Irish market, and the sales now attract buyers and sellers from many quarters and from the worlds of both Flat racing and jumping.

'Hold my bag.
That might be the
next Best Mate in
there.' Viewing at
Doncaster sales.

Ken Oliver, who rode in point-to-points, including for Willie Stephenson, took five Scottish Grand Nationals as a trainer and is well remembered for the placings of Wyndburgh in the Grand National.

On Doncaster's opening day in 2002, a striking brown four-year-old gelding, by Roselier out of Best Mate's dam Katday, was the focus of attention. He was to be named Inexorable. The success of Best

Mate ensured there would be much interest and brisk bidding and by the time Henry Beeby's hammer came down a new record had been established. At 185,000 guineas, Inexorable was the most expensive National Hunt store horse ever sold. He remains the most expensive four-year-old although the following year a three-year-old half-brother of See More Business realised 200,000 guineas.

By the summer of 2004, Inexorable had won three of his six starts in Ireland and is learning all the time. Also the winner of a point-to-point, his trainer David Wachman plans to send him steeplechasing in the 2004–05 season.

∿

Summer racing began in 1995. The season used to end on the first weekend of June with the *Horse and Hound* Cup meeting at Stratford-upon-Avon in the afternoon and Market Rasen that evening, and did not restart until late July. Not only was the ground likely to be firm for jumpers then, but also most of them would be turned out for the summer holidays – and it gave jockeys and trainers a break in which to take a holiday, too. The new summer fixtures were part of an initial two-year trial by the Race Planning Committee designed to maximise competition, using well-watered, accessible Midlands locations, plus Perth in Scotland.

In June 2002, in the early, quiet stage of the season, Jim Culloty injured his right arm again, when falling at Huntingdon. It was to affect him for a long time to come.

15

SEASON 2002–03:
THREE RUNS, THREE WINS

'Knight Attacks Kempton over "Disgraceful" Going' shouted the headline in a *Racing Post* article on 27 October 2002:

Henrietta Knight warned Kempton that dramatic improvement will be required in the track's grass cover if Best Mate is to take part in the Pertemps King George VI Chase after withdrawing her three runners from yesterday's meeting because the ground was 'an absolute disgrace'.

'There's absolutely no grass here…and it's yellow. The grass won't grow between now and the end of the year, so what's it going to be like on King George day? I won't be running Best Mate if there isn't a dramatic improvement in the grass cover.'

This was a stern warning – one could almost say back to the school-marm – from Henrietta Knight, but she would not have made it had she not felt strongly about it. United Racecourse chairman Andrew Wates promised to get it right for the rest of the season.

At this stage, Best Mate's fans had almost another month to wait to see him again. What a season it was to be – only three runs, but three wins, two of them in the top two non-handicap English steeplechases.

It was such a dry autumn that many trainers delayed running their most valuable horses, and in the end that included Best Mate. The Haldon Gold Cup at Exeter brought together some exciting chasers but not its holder. West Lockinge was represented instead by Edredon Bleu – and on ground officially 'good', he saw off the nearest of his four rivals, Seebald, by ten lengths at a generous starting price of 10–1. Two years later, at almost twelve years old, he was to prove an even more impressive substitute when Best Mate bypassed the King George at Kempton for the Ericsson Chase in Ireland – but that is still to come.

A few more weeks into November, Best Mate was entered for the valuable Peterborough Chase at Huntingdon. This was the race that Edredon Bleu had made his own but this time news of Best Mate's entry appeared to have scared off the opposition and entries were re-opened. The ground was given officially as good to soft, but still only five runners went to post. One was an intriguing French entry, Douze Douze, from Guillaume Macaire, who showed splendid enterprise in being willing to take on Best Mate. It was neither the first nor the last time he has been prepared to take on, and sometimes beat, the best the British have to offer and it is refreshing to see a challenge being tackled head-on rather than evaded.

An upbeat Jim Culloty was full of confidence and he rode Best Mate beautifully in the race. The crowd at Huntingdon were aware that they were likely to have just three opportunities to see the rising – or rather risen – star that year, and what they saw that day was the epitome of the perfect racehorse. He looked magnificent. There were no rough edges to be honed and he jumped far better than his French rival, who was trying to get to know the English-style fences before tackling the King George at Kempton on Boxing Day.

French steeplechase fences tend to be slightly higher and wider than the English counterparts, but much, much softer, so that horses brush through them far lower down, a habit that would spell calamity over British fences. They are also upright, with a take-off rail on both sides so that they can be jumped in either direction.

In the race, Best Mate could not be faulted. Apart from Douze Douze, a huge horse, the talented Geos, winner of the King George as a five-year-old in 2000, was running. Although the ground was a bit

Willie Mullins,
trainer of Florida
Pearl, makes his
point.

sticky, Best Mate set the pace for the two mile five furlong event and, jumping well within himself, galloped to a convincing eight-length victory over the French horse.

It had been a true test and Best Mate was back in his full glory.

Guillaume Macaire set about working on his horse's jumping and promised the rematch in the King George would be closer. As far as the bookmakers were concerned, they were looking ahead to Cheltenham. No horse had won two Gold Cups since L'Escargot in 1970 and 1971, but they were shortening Best Mate's price to do so.

Best Mate's next port of call was the King George and there were only five weeks between Huntingdon and the Christmas spectacle. Several horses were being touted as possible winners apart from Best Mate, who had been beaten 'by a better horse' the previous year.

Florida Pearl, the Willie Mullins-trained Irish horse, was set to run again. Another high-class prospect was Bacchanal and, intriguingly, the reigning Queen Mother Champion Two Mile chaser Flagship Uberalles was stepping up to three miles for the first time. A top-class race was in prospect and Jim Culloty was eagerly anticipating it when, for the second successive year, fate intervened.

On 13 December, thirteen days before the big race, Jim was found guilty of dropping his hands and losing third place in a bumper at Doncaster. He was suspended for three days, including Boxing Day. It was a dreadful blow – ironic, too, considering that for 362 days of the year Best Mate does not run.

The services of Andrew Coonan, top Irish solicitor and friend of Henrietta Knight's, were enlisted. If Jim lodged an appeal, he risked having his suspension increased to anything up to ten days, but losing Boxing Day must have felt like ten to him anyway. He went ahead and lodged the appeal.

It was set for 19 December in Portman Square, the London head-quarters of the Jockey Club. The building has a forbidding air to many of those facing a hearing, but the procedure has been fairer since the Ryan Price/Hill House affair of 1967–68, when it was found that the horse manufactured his own dope. Since then, anyone facing a disciplinary hearing has been allowed legal representation.

The day of the appeal arrived and the first thing Andrew Coonan did was to apply for was an adjournment because 'previous commitments' prevented Mr Coonan attending. The request was turned down. Jim Culloty was away riding at Exeter, and therefore the suspension remained. Jim would miss riding Best Mate in the King George. Once is bad enough, but twice was devastating.

Jockey Club spokesman John Maxse said, 'The disciplinary panel makes every effort to hold inquiries at times that cause the least inconvenience for all parties – indeed, the afternoon kick-off for the Culloty hearing was designed to allow time for Mr Coonan to get to London from Ireland.

'I have considerable sympathy for Jim Culloty but I think it is fair

Martin Pipe gave Tony McCoy the go-ahead to take the ride on Best Mate in the 2002 King George.

to say that he did not help his cause by riding at Exeter instead of attending his own appeal hearing.

'Finally, the fact that he did not attend, and that the appeal was withdrawn as soon as the application for an adjournment had been formally rejected, suggests the primary reason for lodging the appeal was not to contest the original finding at Doncaster but rather to seek to put the appeal process temporarily on hold.'

In other words, he thought it a ploy – but who could blame him?

For trainer and owner, the hunt was now on for a replacement jockey. Tony McCoy was favoured, but he was likely to be required to ride either Wahiba Sands or Shooting Light for his boss Martin Pipe in the same race.

In the end, Martin Pipe released Tony McCoy, booking two of his

aspiring jockeys, Rodi Greene and Tom Scudamore (grandson of Grand National-winning Michael and son of multiple champion Peter) for his horses. So it was that Tony McCoy had the leg-up in the big race on an afternoon when he beat his own record for riding the fastest 200 winners in one season.

Some considered the champion had made one of his rare mistakes the previous year in his tactics on Best Mate, others that Florida Pearl was a better horse, but no one was considering this to be a two-horse race. In the end, it belonged to just one.

Eighteen thousand people flocked through Kempton's Sunbury-on-Thames gates that day. The track is totally different from Cheltenham – flat, sharp, right-handed and on sandy soil. The infinite variety of the courses is part of the attraction of British and Irish racing. In other parts of the world, tracks are uniformly the same, even to going the same way round. In Britain and Ireland, some tracks suit a long-striding, galloping horse, others a nippy, handy one; some have a circuit of a mile, others are nearly two miles round; some have tougher fences than others where jumping prowess is rewarded, others have steep hills to test stamina. Some horses go better left-handed than right and vice-versa. Pretty Fontwell in Sussex, uniquely since the demise of Windsor's jumping, has a steeplechase course set out in a figure of eight.

The going for the 2002 King George was soft, in which Best Mate is said to flounder, although Kempton, with its sandy soil, was unlikely to resemble glue. Nevertheless, Best Mate had to work hard. Brilliant on good ground, he now had to dig deeper if he was to prove himself a warrior, and he did. Tony McCoy, anxious not to repeat the previous year's mistake of leaving him too much to do, when he believed Best Mate's stamina might be suspect, had him handily placed as first Bacchanal and then Douze Douze made the pace. Best

Best Mate and Tony McCoy battle for the lead in the 2002 King George at Kempton. They went on to win, and so reverse the disappointment of the previous year.

Mate jumped into the front fully five fences from home, closely attended by Florida Pearl. As the previous year's winner dropped back, another trio was poised to pounce – any one of Bacchanal, Marlborough and Native Upmanship was close enough if good enough.

As they turned into the straight and headed for the last two fences, it was Marlborough who challenged. For probably the first time in his life, Best Mate felt the sting of a whip. Head for head and stride for stride the two horses headed to the last. They jumped it as one. Best Mate was fractionally faster over it and managed to stay ahead to the line, for a winning margin of one and a half lengths.

Tony McCoy was ecstatic while the trainer immediately announced Best Mate would not run again before the Gold Cup.

'Best Mate is the most amazing mover,

the complete athlete. For guts and determination,

that was as good a King George as any I've ever seen.'

Talking post race to the press, Terry Biddlecombe said, 'Good horses should be kept. We don't want to burn them out. Best Mate is the most amazing mover, the complete athlete. For guts and determination, that was as good a King George as any I've ever seen.'

The welcome news for Jim Culloty was that Jim Lewis confirmed the stable jockey would keep the ride on the star.

'I'm not in the business of breaking hearts,' he said, 'and I know Jim would be utterly devastated. I didn't come into racing to do that sort of thing.'

After the race, Best Mate's odds for Cheltenham were cut to between 7–4 and a best-priced 3–1.

So it was a good Christmas for Tony McCoy and one that Jim Culloty would rather forget.

16

BUILD-UP TO CHELTENHAM 2003

In the next two and a half months, on the racecourses of England and Ireland the reputations of various would-be opponents were being made and broken.

Marlborough, a splendid stalwart of Nicky Henderson's Lambourn stable, had staked his claim by running so well to finish second to Best Mate at Kempton. See More Business, third in Best Mate's first Gold Cup at 40–1 and the winner in 1999, was likely to run again. Increasingly, a horse called Hussard Collonges, an eight-year-old trained by Peter Beaumont in Yorkshire, was being tipped as a challenger. Paul Nicholls had a well-regarded eight-year-old in Valley Henry and, in Ireland, Ted Walsh's Commanche Court, second in 2002, was bidding to go one better. First Gold, who had won the King George back in 2000, could not be left out of the reckoning, even though he was likely to be an outsider.

Jim Culloty, meanwhile, remained positive about his mount. He had thought he would win in 2002, but for 2003, he was certain. He told Tom O'Ryan in the *Racing Post* that he was:

…going into this Gold Cup the very same way as I did last year. I'd be very anxious to get everything right, work things out in my head; to know what everyone in the race is likely to do and to have every horse weighed up, which is what you'd do, anyway, riding a short-priced favourite.

There are dangers in every race – anything can happen – but when you're on a horse you think should win, it's up to you to make sure he gets a clear round and to put him in a winning position.

Best Mate travels, settles and jumps – long or short [meaning standing back from the fence and pinging it in full flight or, if meeting it slightly wrong, putting in a short stride] – so in every way you couldn't ask for a more perfect racehorse.

Because he's so well balanced, he's a better horse if you sit still on him at a fence – you'd only unbalance him if you bullied him or fired him in. He's happier working it out for himself.

Jim admitted he was more content in himself now as a rider and not so likely to let a bad run get him down any more, but added, 'A jockey, when he's riding, is always working, always in the spotlight. You can never relax or rest on your laurels in this game.' To do so spells something going wrong. 'You're only as good as your last ride.'

Also in the *Racing Post*, on 3 March, ten days before the 2003 Gold Cup, Rodney Masters described Best Mate's preparation at home in Lockinge. It would be identical to the previous year's build-up with two pieces of serious work [on the gallops] on the Tuesday and Saturday, a dressage session [part of what makes him so biddable and 'elastic'], a school over fences and a canter in the big field. The field leads up to the Ridgeway, an ancient

Nicky Henderson, trainer of Marlborough, one of Best Mate's rivals in the 2003 Cheltenham Gold Cup.

chalk track that runs from Ivinghoe Beacon in Hertfordshire to Avebury in Wiltshire via Goring, Wantage and Marlborough. Possibly the oldest road in Europe, pre-Stonehenge and before Britain was an island, the Ridgeway is probably the oldest surviving relic from our human past.

Henrietta Knight confirmed that Best Mate was stronger than last year and for that reason 'could be that much better'. Although he does not run often, he 'is so easy to train' that he is always fully fit for his races.

Meanwhile, across the water, another horse was being mentioned in the same breath as Best Mate. Beef or Salmon is a chestnut with a stunted tail. The novice's skilful Co. Tipperary trainer Michael Hourigan was happy to put him straight into 'grown-up' races and in the Ericsson Chase at Leopardstown, run two days after Kempton, Beef or Salmon was catching all the headlines. A year younger than Best Mate, his Ericsson win was his third successive victory that winter. He was eligible for novice chases but Michael Hourigan considered him good enough to go straight into the big time. That way, too, he would not be hampered by novices falling or causing interference in big fields. He had a style of running well off the pace – nearer last than first – being given 'plenty of daylight' in which to see his fences, and then he'd pounce with blistering speed on the run in from the last fence. He was being hailed as the horse to topple the Cheltenham king; it was a little like Arkle and Mill House all over again.

In the Ericsson, on heavy ground, Beef or Salmon beat Colonel Braxton and Harbour Pilot, with the disappointing favourite, First Gold, last. Five weeks later, Beef or Salmon's meteoric rise continued over three miles in the Hennessy at Leopardstown, when he beat the same horses into second and third place.

Owners and trainers in Ireland wondered what they could do to lower the colours of this rising superstar – four runs in steeplechases, four wins, all of them at the highest level. Could he prevent Best Mate winning back-to-back Gold Cups in March?

Could he prevent Best Mate

winning back-to-back Gold Cups in March?

17

A SECOND GOLD CUP

So could Best Mate win two in a row? Many good Gold Cup winners had tried and failed in the years since L'Escargot – Silver Buck, Forgive'N'Forget, Desert Orchid, See More Business and Looks Like Trouble among more than a dozen of them.

For the many people thronging the paddock and pre-parade paddock that dank day, Thursday, 13 March, it was the first glimpse they'd had of the handsome horse in the flesh for twelve months. What they saw was an even stronger looking, more mature horse. He carried his head with an imperious air and walked with an easy, aristocratic swing, his kind eyes alert, his ears pricked and interested.

The official going is good and at 3.15 p.m. fifteen runners face the tapes. As the commentator calls, 'They're off!', the crowd roars and Jim Culloty kick starts Best Mate and then settles him in mid division. Rank outsider Modular leads them over the first. Behrajan, See More Business, Hussard Collonges and Colonel Braxton are close up while right at the back is Youragoodun. Beef or Salmon is in his customary place near the rear.

The runners sail over the second and stream past the packed grandstands and rails. Best Mate and his stable companion Chives are still in mid division as are Harbour Pilot and the French horse First Gold; Trackers Tavern and Commanche Court are further behind. Valley Henry is well placed as they head towards the third, still led by Modular.

Jim Culloty and
Best Mate in action.

Suddenly, a horse is down at the back of the field. The colours are yellow, the cap green. There is a mass groan from the crowd as 10,000 Irishmen, and others who had backed the second favourite, realise that Beef or Salmon is down. It's a nasty looking fall. He rolls over twice, awkwardly, before tottering to his feet. Timmy Murphy, his rider, is disconsolate.

As he was near the back, and the loose horse does not immediately continue with the other runners as often happens, it is unlikely many of the leading riders know he has fallen. They would not expect to see him until the last half-mile of the course, anyway, for 'stalking' is how he is usually ridden.

On his way to his second Gold Cup, and Best Mate's jumping was flawless.

So down towards the water jump they continue, and on to the first open ditch. Marlborough, near the back of the field, is not jumping as well as he can. On they swing, up the hill and over the next open ditch, and the formidable fence at the top of the hill, before rolling on to the notorious downhill fence that will be the third last next time round. Best Mate is in the middle and most of the field could be covered by the proverbial handkerchief. Only Youragoodun has not been able to stick with them as See More Business and Behrajzan lead them out on the second circuit.

Still with it all to do,
Best Mate powers on.

Best Mate has Commanche Court, First Gold, Trackers Tavern and Marlborough behind him while Chives has made a significant forward move and is running a big race towards the outside, jumping like a buck.

They're climbing the far hill for the last time and Best Mate jumps his way into sixth place. Jim Culloty is sitting motionless on him, and as they head downhill Chives takes over the lead, sprinting four lengths clear, with Best Mate now fourth.

In a flash, the whole complexion of the race changes. From being a

Best Mate wins his second Gold Cup, with the rest of the field at least ten lengths behind.

dozen horses well placed, four draw clear, Chives, Valley Henry, Behrajan and Best Mate. Valley Henry blunders and his jockey shakes his reins at him but his chance has gone. Behrajan drops back, too, but Trackers Tavern moves forward.

And then there were two, the stable companions, Chives and Best Mate, but not for long. Best Mate cruises effortlessly into the lead. It has been many a long year since class of this sort has been so dominant in a Gold Cup. He is drawing further and further away and there are still two fences left to jump. Then there was one fence between Best Mate and history.

Collective hearts in mouths there may be, but with no need. Best Mate simply soars over the last, taking it in his stride as smoothly and perfectly as is possible, with not a semblance of a mistake, not a moment's hesitation. He storms up the final hill towards the winning post, still pulling away.

'Simply the best, Best Mate,' calls the commentator, almost drowned out by the roaring cheers of the crowds.

'Simply the best, Best Mate,' calls the commentator, almost drowned out by the roaring cheers of the crowds.

Best Mate's superiority made it look so easy, yet he was running against the very best that England, France and Ireland could line up beside him.

It was a case of Best Mate first and the rest nowhere but, for the record, Trackers Tavern stayed on into second, a full ten lengths behind the winner, with the dour Harbour Pilot third and a length behind him, finishing fourth, Valley Henry. Next came Behrajan with Commanche Court in sixth. Chives, who put up such a splendid display for so long, was seventh and then there was a gap back to gallant See More Business, followed by Youragoodun, Colonel Braxton and Marlborough, who was near the rear throughout, and finally the

200–1 outsider and early leader Modular. Beef or Salmon was the only faller and both Hussard Collonges and the disappointing First Gold pulled up.

And there, running down the horse-walk to greet each other, are Henrietta Knight and Terry Biddlecombe, having watched – or not, in Henrietta's case – from different places. They hug and welcome in their super hero, Best Mate.

Naturally enough, the press were ecstatic after this victory, reflecting the public view of it as well as the racing industry's. Ted Walsh, who presents racing for RTE viewers in Ireland as well as having trained Commanche Court, said Best Mate 'is right up there with the very best Gold Cup winners I can remember and he could get even better.'

Michael Hourigan, trainer of the highly regarded Beef or Salmon, agreed. 'He couldn't have done it any better.'

Peter Thomas, writing in the *Racing Post*, was prophetic:

Best Mate looks every inch a great steeplechaser and fortunately he was snapped up by genuinely likeable and sporting connections who recognised that fact very early on.

Anyone not satisfied with this will have to wait a long, long time for it to get any better – unless, of course, you count Best Mate's third Gold Cup win in twelve months' time.

For those of us of a certain age, who just missed out on Arkle and have spent the last thirty years hearing about how wonderful he was, this was the moment we had all been waiting for. Best Mate looks every inch a great steeplechaser and fortunately he was snapped up by genuinely likeable and sporting connections who recognised that fact very early on. He and they have silenced the doubters in the best possible manner, rising to each new challenge with style, class and magnanimity – the only hint of arrogance coming from the horse himself.

Arklc, in isolated splendour as he soars to his second Gold Cup.

Praising Best Mate as 'a real champion who has crept up on us', David Ashforth wrote, also in the *Racing Post*:

Funny that it's taken so long to stop treating Best Mate merely as a very good horse, and to start celebrating him as a great one.

It's taken time partly because he's not exuberantly flamboyant. Best Mate doesn't dominate and devour rivals and fences; like a perfect athlete, he glides and floats and smooths his way from one fence to the next, from one side to the other. He doesn't show off; it just naturally comes easy.

It was a very good description. In one way, Best Mate was similar to L'Escargot, who apart from his two Gold Cups also won the top handicaps of the Grand National and Irish National, carrying top weight in both; yet he was seldom referred to as a great from the past.

The same could be said of Cottage Rake who, like Arkle, won three Gold Cups. Although there are few people alive today who remember him, those who do often say that because he had the speed to win on the Flat, he might have had the class to outpace Arkle from the last fence, had they ever met. However, one thing Best Mate has underlined is that we can only speculate on how champions of different generations might have fared had they been running in the same era as each other.

After the race, some people bemoaned how little would be seen of

L'Escargot, another two-times winner of the Gold Cup.

Dawn Run, one of Best Mate's illustrious forerunners, and the only horse to have won both the Champion Hurdle and the Gold Cup.

the champion by the public in the future. David Ashforth, after his unreserved praise of the horse, commented:

It's hard to argue with a trainer as admirable and obviously competent as Henrietta Knight, who knows Best Mate and has trained him to a Gold Cup double and a lifetime record of eleven wins and five seconds from sixteen starts, but we ought to ask why the best china in the country's cupboard can only be brought out three times a year? …

Times have changed but not all in the direction of more demanding races. Thanks partly to Cheltenham's much improved drainage, Thursday's Gold Cup was run in less testing conditions than former champions have often faced.

Champions promote a sport. If Best Mate is to give jump racing the boost it craves, we need to see him more than three times a year. What can be done to tempt him out?

This article sparked a lively debate in the letters pages, as well as prompting correspondence from those who still considered it ludicrous to mention Best Mate in the same breath as Arkle.

What has to be remembered is that the person in charge, with the day-to-day hands-on care and knowledge of the horse, is the only one who really knows what is best for it. Thoroughbreds are inclined to be highly strung, delicate creatures, some more so than others, and it could be that by taking a horse such as Best Mate to the well too often, he could become over-charged, too hyped up and excited. Back in 1986, there was such an incredible reception for Dawn Run in the winner's enclosure at Cheltenham, to this day the only horse to win both a Champion Hurdle and Gold Cup, that it sent her into supercharge. The noise, the jostling, the adulation were such that next time she ran, in a chase at Liverpool, she was so hyped up, reliving all the post-race excitement of her last appearance, that she simply galloped

What has to be remembered is that the person in charge, with the day-to-day hands-on care and knowledge of the horse, is the only one who really knows what is best for it.

The Queen paid her first visit to Cheltenham in fifty years in 2003, and presented owner Jim Lewis with his second Tote Gold Cup. Henrietta Knight, Terry Biddlecombe and Jim Culloty look on.

into the first fence and never took off at all. Although she went on to win a special match race against her long-time opponent Buck House in Ireland, sadly she was to miss one out again later that year in France, breaking her neck instantly in a fatal fall.

The trainer's approach must be respected, and spectators will look forward all the more to Best Mate's appearances when he does make them.

Gold Cup day had begun in a very special way that year. Her Majesty the Queen, paying her first visit to Cheltenham for fifty years, unveiled a portrait bust of her mother in the unsaddling enclosure before racing began.

Cheltenham's chairman, Lord Vestey, welcomed Her Majesty and said, 'The Queen Mother's love of Cheltenham touched the lives of many people, in moments of victory and disappointment.' He said National Hunt racing had grown immensely in popularity in that half century and that 'this is due, to a great extent, to the very close association the sport enjoyed with Queen Elizabeth the Queen Mother over so many years.'

The splendid Desert Orchid, winner of the 1989 Gold Cup and just as popular as ever with the public, and his lass Janice Coyle, were presented to the Queen. Several winning jockeys were also in the line-up – Martin Molony (Silver Fame 1951), Willie Robinson (Mill House 1963), Fred Winter (Saffron Tartan and Mandarin 1961 and 1962), Paddy Mullins (Dawn Run 1986) and Tony McCoy (Mr Mulligan 1997). Record-breaking trainer Martin Pipe was there too. Fred Winter, who sadly died in June 2004, trained 1978's victor, Midnight Court. Another winning trainer presented to Her Majesty was Michael Dickinson, who had the first five home in 1983, headed by Bregawn. He also trained the 1982 winner Silver Buck.

How fitting that the Queen, who had had a short-lived association with National Hunt racing when sharing Monaveen with her mother for two seasons from 1949–50 before turning her attentions to the Flat, should, on her return, witness one of the great Gold Cup results.

So Best Mate took his long annual summer holiday, when he could amble around, resting, frolicking, relaxing, enjoying the grass and the peace, and the break from training routine. In September, Henrietta decided to hold an Open Day so that the horse's admirers could see the champion at home, a magnanimous and thoughtful gesture that led to some 3,000 people visiting when the due date came round.

Henrietta Knight leads out Best Mate at the West Lockinge Open Day in September 2003.

18

SEASON 2003–04:
THE BEST-LAID PLANS...

The lovely Best Mate returned to training, carrying the hopes of all those people who wanted him to continue his winning sequence. At eight, rising nine, years old, he could be expected to be at his peak. He was unbeaten in 2002-03 and the planned route this time was the same as before – the Peterborough Chase at Huntingdon in November, the King George at Kempton on Boxing Day and the attempt to become a triple champion at Cheltenham in March.

The annual stable tour by the *Racing Post*'s Rodney Masters in October revealed that Best Mate was, according to Henrietta Knight, 'in tremendous form and Terry believes he has come on again since last season. He's certainly stronger, particularly in his neck, and he's in better condition now than he was at this stage last year.'

She added that the King George could be difficult to win 'if the likes of First Gold, Jair du Cochet and several of the speed merchants are on top form.' Her prediction was proved correct sooner than anticipated.

Before his first race at Huntingdon, one or two warning signals flashed. Jim Culloty, usually upbeat, suggested the horse could be 'vulnerable' round such a sharp track. Huntingdon is a flat course, typical of the East Anglian countryside, with no hill to bring out Best Mate's stamina and to sap the speed horses.

Then the weather changed, affecting the going. In the week before

Jacques Ricou on Jair du Cochet, the pair who beat Best Mate on his seasonal reappearance at Huntingdon in November 2003.

the race, the ground was 'the fast side of good', but 4mm of rain fell the night before the race.

Fitness was not a problem. Best Mate had won first time out every year he had ever raced and was not one of those horses that needed a race to bring him to peak fitness; that could be done at home, and it was. He was reported as being 'one hundred per cent ready'.

Paul Nicholls believed that his horse, Valley Henry, might topple the champion, reporting that he had 'bags of toe…I expect a big run.' Valley Henry was considered the 'value bet' by some tipsters.

Another in the field was La Landiere, a remarkable mare, coming to the race unbeaten in her previous seven runs. Although her trainer Richard Phillips did not expect her to beat Best Mate, at least one racing tipster thought it possible.

Trainer Guillaume
Macaire gives his
instructions to jockey
Jacques Ricou.

Guillaume Macaire also believed the great horse could be beaten. He was the trainer of Jair du Cochet, a young horse with huge potential.

'It would be very arrogant to say he will beat Best Mate, but there's a chance,' said Macaire, who was in England to acclimatise the horse to English fences ahead of the King George. He certainly achieved that – his horse won.

Lowering the colours of Best Mate was in many ways a sad occasion, yet Best Mate maintained his record of never being out of the first two, which is in itself incredible.

The defeat was blamed on the mud. Several breeding and racing people who know about these things say, simply, that horses sired by Un Desperado do not go in soft ground. Best Mate did not show his usual fluency and that is why – he was 'stuck in the mud'.

The pace was not excessive but still Best Mate struggled and Jair du Cochet came home a comfortable winner, in spite of hitting the last fence. He finished eight lengths ahead of Best Mate, with Valley Henry one and three-quarter lengths behind in third and La Landiere fourth.

In press reports afterwards, Henrietta Knight was quoted as saying, 'Best Mate can't use his beautiful action when it's like that – but take nothing away from Jair du Cochet, who is a very good horse. Best Mate was one hundred per cent fit today. That wasn't a problem at all, it was just the ground. It was horrible out there. He had to be beaten sometime, didn't he? I'd rather it was today than at Cheltenham.'

Sadly, Jair du Cochet did not survive for Cheltenham, three and a half months away. He was tragically killed at home in France

Then came the big surprise. It was announced that Best Mate might miss the King George altogether and go for the Ericsson Chase in Leopardstown, Ireland, instead.

shortly before the scheduled re-match with Best Mate in the 2004 Gold Cup.

The same afternoon as the Peterborough Chase at Huntingdon, what turned out to be a significant race was run at Ascot when Andrew Thornton, riding Kingscliff, produced a wonderful feat of horsemanship, one that stands comparison with the greatest in the annals of steeplechasing. It rivalled Fred Winter's ride in Auteuil on Mandarin (broken bit) and Tim Brookshaw's on Wyndburgh in the Grand National (broken stirrup). A rein broke and for almost all the race Kingscliff ran unsteered – and he won. He was ante-post second favourite for the 2004 Cheltenham Gold Cup but did not run because his trainer, Robert Alner, believed he was a little below par. Now Kingscliff is being seriously considered as a rival to Best Mate for the 2005 Gold Cup.

Press reaction to Best Mate's defeat was mixed, ranging from 'good horse though he is, he wasn't quite good enough to win at Huntingdon on Saturday', 'it's got to be his worst display since novice days' and it represented 'nothing more than a reality check', to 'Just a hiccup – but it means that Best Mate will really have to fight in the King George'. Some felt it was not a bad thing for him to be beaten, if only to encourage more horses to take him on in future.

Then came the big surprise. It was announced that Best Mate might miss the King George altogether and go for the Ericsson Chase in Leopardstown, Ireland, instead.

The stable's stalwart, Edredon Bleu, incidentally, had won at Clonmel in Ireland the day before Huntingdon at the start of what was to be an incredible season even by his evergreen standards.

The question of whether Best Mate would run in England or Ireland was tossed about and debated up and down the land. Meanwhile, other potential Cheltenham Gold Cup prospects came into the picture. Novice Therealbandit trained by Martin Pipe might side-step the Sun Alliance Novices Chase and go straight for the Gold Cup; and Beef or Salmon, who had been on the sidelines with mucus in his lungs, was reported back on track. One regular, former winner See More Business, would definitely not be there – in early January he went into honourable retirement.

Finally, the Best Mate Christmas decision was made. He would bypass the King George and head for the Ericsson in Ireland. Edredon Bleu would be his substitute at Kempton.

Some understudy! Edredon Bleu may have been a week away from his official twelfth birthday, and he may have started at 25–1 against First Gold, Jair du Cochet and co., but no one told him he was meant to be an ageing outsider. He had won all three of his previous races that season and, in a truly emotional race, he stormed away with the King George, from Tiutchev, First Gold, Fondmort and Marlborough. The mare, La Landiere, finished sixth and the only other finisher was the quietly fancied Swansea Bay. Both Valley Henry and Le

With Best Mate giving the King George a miss, Jim Culloty took stablemate Edredon Bleu to win the race – it was some compensation for having missed out on a ride in the previous two years.

Roi Miguel fell but the real mystery of the race was Jair du Cochet, who was pulled up.

As for Edredon Bleu, he was also to win his final outing of the season in February, making it five in a row. Michael Moore, the 'spotter' from Co. Cork, echoed the feelings of many when he said, 'What Edredon Bleu has done is phenomenal. He is in many ways the opposite to Best Mate in that he thrives on racing and he loves to get into a battle.'

The decision to route Best Mate to Leopardstown caused a certain amount of controversy among the armchair 'trainers' who claimed it had nothing to do with the ground at Kempton and everything to do with taking the easier option, avoiding the hotter opponents. Henrietta was going back on her word over plans for her horse, they said.

The truth was, of course, that Henrietta, as always, had only her horse's best interests at heart. It was not, she said, an easy decision, but she and Terry felt the ground conditions were not perfect at Kempton. The ground staff had watered the course and tried to get it good but there were still some firmer patches. Writing in the *Daily Telegraph*, she revealed that two years previously Best Mate had been considerably jarred when beaten by Florida Pearl there.

He suffered from sore shins and muscular problems in his shoulders. It took six weeks for him to come right. In that year, the ground still had an element of frost in it beneath the surface and this bony layer had stumped up our horse. The ground at Kempton in the run-up to this year's race also possesses an element of jar and the prospect of injuring Best Mate again by racing him on ground [that] is not ideal has made us turn our backs on the Boxing Day showpiece.

England's loss was to be Ireland's gain and there, in the luxury of Leopardstown, some 20,000 people squeezed through the turnstiles for their big Christmas racing festival and to welcome Best Mate back to the land of his birth. It was a tremendous occasion for Irish racing Early in the morning, Best Mate's connections walked the course and found the ground perfect. 'Spotter' Michael Moore was with them and, later in the day, breeder Jacques Van't Hart was among the watching crowds.

Leopardstown is probably Ireland's smartest track and, since the demise of Phoenix Park, the only one near Dublin, being six miles south of the city centre towards the Dublin Mountains, with the M50 running adjacent to it.

In a line-up of Ireland's best, only Harbour Pilot was missing, due to sickness, but most considered it a two-horse race between Best Mate and Beef or Salmon.

Robert Hall of RTE put it to Terry Biddlecome in a pre-race interview, 'There were lots of decisions about coming?'

'Were there?' replied Terry. 'Not on our part. We walked the course at Kempton and thought it would suit Edredon Bleu better than Matey.'

Asked how he compared Best Mate and Arkle, Terry replied, 'Times are different. Arkle was outstanding but so far Best Mate has done everything asked of him, with a bit of a blip last time in very soft ground.'

In response to a question on how few runs per year Best Mate has, Terry said, 'He's a young horse. Everyone wants to see him last. They don't want to see him burnt out. Look at Edredon Bleu. He's been racing from four to twelve because he doesn't have too many races. People want to see them.'

'But only four times since his first Gold Cup win?' queried Robert Hall.

'Yep, plenty,' replied Terry.

Before the start, the two 'gladiators', jockeys Timmy Murphy and Jim Culloty, spoke of the race ahead.

'It's a great day for Irish racing,' said Timmy, who would be riding Beef or Salmon, winner of this race a year ago.

Jim admitted that the Peterborough Chase at Huntingdon had not gone to plan. 'There was rain from 4 a.m. to 4 p.m. We were in the fifth race and by then the ground was bottomless. He needs a big galloping, jumping track like Cheltenham and we're hoping for that here.'

So the stage was set. Owner Jim Lewis walked with Best Mate and his lass, Jackie Jenner, in the pre-parade ring, where a wintry sun filtered through the surrounding palm-like fronds of the yucca trees. Then it was on into the parade ring where crowds eight to ten deep pressed for a view. Best Mate might be the English-owned and trained champion, but he was born in Ireland and the Irish had come to see him.

In the middle of the paddock Henrietta, smartly dressed as always and sporting a warm winter hat, was laughing and smiling broadly with the two Jims, Lewis and Culloty, and then it was a leg-up from Terry for the jockey.

Best Mate looked magnificent; his muscles rippled in the sun and his coat shone. He looked all over the perfect racehorse, lean, fit, trained to the moment – and he was. As he cantered past the stands, his tail flowing majestically behind him, his head held proud, his neck arched, his action superb, the crowd applauded; but there was louder applause for Beef or Salmon, the local hero.

Beef or Salmon was out to redeem himself but this was Best Mate's

Then it was on into the parade ring where crowds eight to ten deep pressed for a view. Best Mate might be the English-owned and trained champion, but he was born in Ireland and the Irish had come to see him.

day. He simply took the race by storm and looked as impressive as he had in his second Cheltenham Gold Cup. He looked invincible. It was one of those days when you leave the track knowing you have seen a great horse and revelling in it. You might see the detail closer up on the television, but nothing matches the buzz of actually being there.

Best Mate went out for a stroll. Always handy and never out of third gear, jumping superbly and economically, he was tracking Colonel Braxton with about a mile go. Beef or Salmon, the darling of the Irish and holder of this race, was behind him in third but never looked a danger. At the second last, with Tony McCoy at work on Colonel Braxton, Jim popped Best Mate up his inside, gathered him together

and strolled into the lead. Once round the home turn, all Jim Culloty had to do was let Best Mate out a little and the result was stirring. Best Mate soared over the last and sprinted up the run-in as if he had wings, with Jim Culloty looking over his shoulder several times probably in disbelief at the non-existent challenges. Le Coudray came through to

finish second and Beef or Salmon, who gurgled during the race, was third. Over a million euros were taken in bets that memorable afternoon.

What a convincing way it was for Best Mate to come back from defeat on his seasonal debut at Huntingdon. Jim Culloty said afterwards that the other runners had gone too slowly for him.

'I had to slow Best Mate down, but once I let him go after the second last he sprinted. He's absolutely in a different class. I could go down to a fence with my eyes closed – hope that doesn't come back to haunt me. He's twice the horse on decent ground.'

Henrietta Knight confessed she had not watched the race but had listened to it while walking round the car parks.

'I have never known Terry so nervous before a race, we were coming into unknown territory, but the ground was perfect. He may

Best Mate in action during the Ericsson Chase in Leopardstown.

Best Mate heads for home in the Ericsson at Leopardstown, after giving Kempton a miss.

Owner Jim Lewis congratulates his jockey on a remarkable victory at Leopardstown.

not be Arkle, but he's some horse. People say they don't see enough of him, but they can come and see him at home, we're giving several opportunities in January and February.'

Jim Lewis thanked the Irish for the welcome given to them.

So Jim Culloty had still not ridden Best Mate in the King George – although he had just won it on board Edredon Bleu – but no doubt winning the Ericsson in his home country instead was sweeter still.

Best Mate was now on target for a third Cheltenham Gold Cup.

19

ALL IN THE FAMILY

Christmas 2003 was remarkable. Three of Katday's progeny won graded races. Best Mate, the king, won the Grade 1 Ericsson Chase at Leopardstown on 28 December, and the very next day his two years younger full brother Cornish Rebel won the Grade 1 Challow Hurdle at Newbury ridden by Ruby Walsh for trainer Paul Nicholls and owner Graham Roach. Their six-year-old half-brother, Inexorable, won the Grade 3 Dorans Pride Novices Hurdle at Limerick on the same day as the Ericsson for trainer David Wachman and owner Gigginstown House Stud in the hands of M.D. Grant.

Alfred Buller presents the Irish Thoroughbred Breeders Association Broodmare of 2003 Award jointly to Best Mate's breeder Jacques Van't Hart (left) and Philip Myerscough, now the owner of Best Mate's dam, Katday.

Katday, Best Mate's mother, and foal with owner Philip Myerscough.

In February 2004, Best Mate's breeder Jacques Van't Hart and Philip Myerscough of Baroda Stud, who now owns Katday, were jointly awarded the prize for the National Champion Broodmare 2003 in a touching gesture by the Irish Thoroughbred Breeders Association at its annual dinner.

Any relative of Best Mate's has become much sought after and his only full sister is the most valuable of all. In February 2004, Geoffrey Rowe, owner of a burgeoning Devon stud and better known as the comedian Jethro to his millions of fans, travelled to Baroda Stud on the edge of the Curragh in Co. Kildare to see her.

A lifelong follower of hounds, mostly by car, Jethro took an interest in show horses in about 1994 and this led to him being invited to judge the in-hand classes at a show in Northern Ireland in 2001. There he met and lunched with the ridden-hunter judge Alan Munnis, who extolled the virtues of Thoroughbred breeding. The two got on famously and Jethro remarked that he might like a couple of Thoroughbred brood mares. 'But I only want the best,' he added.

Two and a half years after that show, with the help of Alan Munnis and fellow Northern Irishman Alfred Buller, Jethro had assembled as fine a band of National Hunt brood mares as it is possible to imagine. He owned a full sister to the champion staying hurdler Baracouda, a half-sister to the ill-fated Jair du Cochet, one of only six horses ever to have beaten Best Mate, and a half-sister to Shotgun Willie, a half-sister to Mini Sensation (who won the Welsh Grand National), a half-sister to Azertyop, the 2004 Queen Mother Two Mile Champion Chaser. He had a half-sister to Galway Man and La Landiere, and had acquired the lovely grey mare Absaloms Lady, winner of twenty-three races, Miss Orchestra, winner of the Midlands Grand National, and Mistinguett, second in the Triumph Hurdle and half-sister to Sinntara. He also has Queen's Flagship, who is a full sister to Flagship Uberalles and half-sister to Viking Flagship. Those were more than most people could even dream of.

'Some people try to swing the lead,' Jethro commented when I went to see him in June 2004. 'I simply turn them down and look

Jethro with Best Mate's sister Flying Iris (left) and Pechaubar, full sister to Baracouda.

elsewhere. I've been very, very lucky, often being in the right place at the right time, and a lot of that is down to Alan and Alfred.'

Then they went for the big one. Jethro takes up the story.

'It's a bit like Elton John's art collection – no one knew he was a collector until he bought the big one. Then it was public knowledge. It's been a bit like that with me.'

He went to look at a half-sister to Best Mate at Eddie O'Grady's but, 'We got delayed on the way, drinking Irish whiskey, and the next day she was away galloping somewhere, so we never made it.'

He did make it, though, to Baroda Stud to see the three-year-old Flying Iris. Already bigger than Best Mate was at that age, the filly had thrived for Philip and Jane Myerscough and was lightly broken when Jethro visited with Alfred Buller.

'I remember telling Jethro she could win in the show-ring,' recalled Philip Myerscough, a director of Tattersalls (Ireland), 'but like a lot of Un Desperado's offspring, she swings a foot, and he immediately said she wouldn't win with that. I knew then that there were no flies on him.'

The respect was mutual and it took about six hours to haggle over the price, by which time Jethro was almost back on the ferry, but the deal was done. Best Mate's full sister Flying Iris would be coming to Devon, via a visit to Alfred Buller's Scarva House Stud in Northern Ireland, where she would be covered by Exit to Nowhere. Jethro wasn't tempted to run her, fine racehorse though she would probably have been.

'It's just not worth the risk if she were to break a leg,' he explained.

She is the only full sister and so it was straight to breeding rather than risk a racecourse accident.

Jethro's stud is kept immaculately and he is very involved with its first-class husbandry. A carpenter by trade until a little bit of singing and storytelling in local pubs in his native Cornwall sent him zooming into the stratosphere, he was doing some carpentry when I arrived for my visit.

He showed me the mares one Sunday morning, nine in the field, five of them lying down. Best Mate's sister was the last to get up, and Jethro stroked her. She is a big filly, a lighter bay than Best Mate with beautiful wide-apart eyes and a conformation that screams 'steeplechaser'. She has a lovely laid-back temperament although she is boss of the rest. The sibling trait of 'I'm the best' is there, but with no kicking or biting, just enough presence to make sure the rest know she is queen.

'Henrietta and Terry were here last week,' said Jethro, 'and reckon of all the relatives, this is the one that looks most like Best Mate.'

Jethro talks to all the horses and is a natural stockman. He is a 'homer'. He likes nothing more than coming home and being among his friends and horses on the edge of Dartmoor, Hawk's Tor in the distance, once his long summer season is over.

'I speak to the mares and young stock and give them cuddles every day I'm here,' he confided in a light West Country lilt, his ever-present curly pipe in mouth or hand, his beard showing flecks of grey.

At seventeen years old, in the summer of 2004 Katday looks a picture. Almost black, the only trace of white on her is an almost indiscernible star on her forehead. She has good clean limbs and doesn't look her age. With a Bob Back foal at foot, she is in foal to Definite Article. Apart from the award from the Irish Thoroughbred Breeders Association, she is also Broodmare of the Year for the Kildare branch.

Philip and Jane Myerscough run a mainly Flat-race stud at Athgarvan on the outskirts of the Curragh, the lovely 5,000 acre, gorse-studded plain that is to Irish racing what Newmarket is to the English industry. They used to breed for the Flat exclusively until they fell for a National Hunt mare called Adariysa by Derby winner Shirley Heights. She was so good looking that Philip bought her, already in foal to Un Desperado, who at that time was completely unknown. The foal had been conceived in France. The result, a colt the Myerscoughs named Ventana Canyon, went on to win the 1996 Arkle Chase at Cheltenham by a stunning twenty lengths.

'I speak to the mares and young stock and give them cuddles every day I'm here,' he confided in a light West Country lilt, his ever-present curly pipe in mouth or hand, his beard showing flecks of grey.

He had been second in the previous year's Supreme Novices Hurdle and when Philip went to the February Goffs Sales in 1996, he was eager to buy another mare in foal to Un Desperado. This was Katday and a month later, she produced the brown colt Inca Trail. Philip Myerscough stayed with Un Desperado and the next year Katday produced another brown colt, Cornish Rebel. A brown colt came along again in 1997, this time by Roselier and named Inexorable.

Sidalcea is a Katday filly by Oscar, and after she won her bumper there were those who told Philip Myerscough he would be 'mad' to run her any more in case of accident. She is now safely in foal to Alflora.

In 2000, with Best Mate having started his winning trail, plus persuasion from Declan Weld and, most importantly, with Philip and

Inca Trail in action at
the Coral Cup
Handicap Hurdle in
March 2004.

Jane Myerscough liking their own two youngsters by Un Desperado, they decided to return Katday to him. That fortuitous mating resulted in the conception of Flying Iris, just months before the stallion's death.

Although Flying Iris looked a great racing prospect, Philip Myerscough understands entirely Jethro's decision to put her straight in foal.

Inca Trail won his first bumper at Naas in January 2002 and, trained by Henrietta Knight for Philip Myerscough, finished a highly encouraging third to Rhinestone Cowboy in the November bumper at Cheltenham's Open meeting. He has also won a hurdle and a chase so far.

Cornish Rebel, trained by Paul Nicholls, has to date won three of

Best Mate's full brother Cornish Rebel, ridden by Ruby Walsh, who won the Challow Hurdle at Newbury the day after Matey's Leopardstown triumph.

his five races, a bumper and two hurdles. He has also, by all accounts, been a bit of a monkey but one who is growing up and being prepared for his next stage in life, steeplechasing.

Inexorable, trained in Ireland by David Wachman, has won three hurdle races from six racecourse appearances. So these two brothers and one half-brother of Best Mate are all showing talent, each of them having won three races. Good though they are, they also have unplaced runs, which is quite normal. Best Mate is the exception to the rule. A first foal is often small and, traditionally, not as good as those that follow, so here again Best Mate is an exception. Although small as a youngster, he has matured into a fine, upstanding and exceptionally good-looking horse.

20

TRIUMPH AND TRAGEDY

The focus throughout January and February 2004 was on the Cheltenham Festival in general and the Gold Cup, with its promise of a Best Mate three-timer, in particular.

As usual, Best Mate did not take part in any of the prep races. Henrietta Knight had more than amply proved that she could prepare him from home.

For the connections of Jair du Cochet, his dress rehearsal came on 26 January in the Pillar Property Chase at Cheltenham, exactly a month after his baffling failure at Kempton. At seven years old, he was two years younger than Best Mate and could be called the pretender – if he could redeem himself after his last run. He did it in style, beating Rince Ri by a convincing six lengths. An exciting Cheltenham battle looked in prospect.

Unfortunately, it was not to be. Nine days before the Gold Cup, Jair du Cochet was having his final serious gallop at home in Les Mathes, France, when, inexplicably, his leg broke. There was no alternative but to put him down. It was a devastating blow and illustrated all too sharply the risk of horse owning, especially as it happened in the relative safety of home.

Natasha Houtcieff, from Guillaume Macaire's establishment, wrote to me in July:

Jair du Cochet in action. He could have been a real threat to Best Mate in the 2004 Gold Cup, but a broken leg a few days before the race meant he had to be put down.

Jair du Cochet was doing his last piece of work before the Cheltenham Festival. He worked brilliantly, slowly building speed and still accelerating past us at the end of his gallop. The tension built up during the morning changed into excitement as Guillaume turned to us and said, 'Now, we go to Cheltenham!' But he had barely finished when the lads nearby circling on the rest of the ring shouted, 'Jair!', pointing to the end of the gallop obscured from our view, where Jacques Ricou had dismounted a stationary Jair du Cochet.

'It was the cruellest blow imaginable. Jair had spontaneous catastrophe fracture of the right cannon [shin bone] at the very end of the gallop. The skin was not broken but there were too many pieces of bone to stabilise surgically and so the very sad decision to put down this lovely horse had to be made.

'Everyone was devastated, especially Guillaume and Jacques Ricou. Guillaume always said Jair was a 'stupid' horse, with some unpredictable reactions. Maybe it was so, as he did not seem distressed by his injury and stood very quietly while all of us were in a state of complete shock.

'Cochet is the name of the stud where Jair was born. Jair seems to be a religious title in the Jewish tradition, but we are not quite sure about that.

'We watched the Gold Cup with Guillaume, of course, but on TV… He was very enthusiastic about Best Mate's win. He thinks Best Mate is a fantastic horse, and as you say we will never know, but the only time Jair du Cochet and Best Mate raced against each other, Jair won.

'… I am sorry but Guillaume has asked me to reply as he still cannot face the loss of his best horse, his 'best mate', as he used to call him!'

At just seven years old and already the winner of thirteen races from twenty-three runs, the bay could have been anything. At the time of Jair's death, Best Mate had won twelve of his eighteen races, and was two years older. Undoubtedly, Jair's death showed the downside of racing.

Meanwhile, extra security measures were being taken to safeguard Best Mate. Infrared cameras were placed in his stable and two guards took turns to watch the pictures from it constantly. A 'spy' camera was erected by the IVS Group to give 360 degree surveillance of the whole area. But the only unusual happenings in West Lockinge were reserved for the postman. Something in the region of 800 good-luck cards were delivered in the days preceding the race – and around the same number again in congratulations in the weeks after.

The day before the Gold Cup, Best Mate schooled over seven fences. Very few trainers allow a horse to jump so close to a race, let alone such an important one, for fear that even a little cut could knock it out of the starting line-up, but this is a part of Henrietta's tradition. It means a horse of hers always comes racing with its 'eye in'.

Best Mate on the way to his hard-fought victory in the totesport Gold Cup in March 2004.

Ten runners were declared for the race and Best Mate was odds-on favourite. There had been other odds-on favourites since Arkle but none had won. For Arkle's third Gold Cup he was an incredible 1–10 – it is impossible to envisage that ever happening again. Best Mate was the hero of the moment, however, and his legion of fans wanted to see him win again.

The trainer had done her bit, and now it was down to Best Mate and his jockey. Jim Culloty had walked the course with Terry Biddle-combe and they had decided to run just a couple of horse widths off the inside rail to get the better ground. That was also the shortest

Best Mate jumps the last and heads for home.

route and so would save precious lengths. The danger was in getting boxed in, which, as we have seen, is exactly what happened, but Jim Culloty extricated his horse from the predicament, fighting all the way up the final furlong to the finishing line. As Best Mate passed the winning post, his jockey raised three fingers in salute, one for each time Best Mate had won the Gold Cup.

In emerging successfully from that tight spot, Best Mate had proved that he was no softie. Far from tamely admitting defeat when boxed in by a rival, he showed true courage, character and commitment in adversity.

'He's tough and was brilliantly ridden,' Henrietta smiled. 'I just can't tell you the relief. It was much worse this year and I couldn't watch the first circuit and a half… It's just an immense relief to see him win because everybody in the country has taken him to their hearts and I couldn't bear to let them all down. But he was better than ever beforehand – in real tip-top form.'

Confirming that plans for 2005 would be the same as before, she added, 'There's only so much mileage in racehorses and I get annoyed by those who criticise us for wrapping Best Mate in cotton wool… By looking after him we are reaping the rewards and he might be even better next year…

'This has been a real ordeal, and I honestly thought we would be beaten at the last, but we saw another side of Best Mate today. We knew he had bags of class and all the ability in the world, but we saw up that famous hill today that he has also got plenty of bottle…

'It's a privilege to be associated with such a good horse. Arkle was a great horse and I refuse to compare different generations, but there is no doubt that Best Mate is the best around.'

'Half a length, that's a mile and a half in paradise,' said Jim Lewis. 'Whatever happens after this, I don't care if I never see another winner in my entire life because everybody wanted him to win.

'It was a huge, huge responsibility for Henrietta Knight. I think the only guy who was confident we were going to win during the race was Jim Culloty. He's one cool dude.'

Terry Biddlecombe chipped in with, 'He's run his guts out today and needs a little rest now. He's done all that's been asked of him… People complain that we wrap him up in cotton wool but we've come here today and won the race… Jim Culloty gave Best Mate a brilliant, brilliant ride. He didn't panic, and he escaped just at the right time… Jim was a perfectionist.'

When asked about the tactics used by Paul Carberry to box him in, Jim Culloty commented, 'I would have done exactly the same in his position…he was just doing his job… It was just a case of not panicking. I knew there was still plenty of time left, Thierry had taken no prisoners up front and we had gone a punishing gallop, so I was sure that they would tire, and I managed finally to pull out going to the second last. That was the crucial fence and he winged it. That effectively sealed the race.

'He has equalled Arkle's record in the race now and I would love to see him come back fit and well and try to better it next year.'

'Of course, I was worried when we were boxed in, but it all ended happily. At the end of the day, it was guts that got us home, and I'm so relieved.'

The bookmakers were losers but for once they didn't mind. Simon Clare of Coral said, 'You simply can't put a figure on what this incredible horse has done for racing's image… Best Mate has reminded us all how thrilling horse-racing can be.'

David Hood from William Hill added, 'It was a score draw really. What a cracking result!'

After the race, Best Mate was quoted at between 5–2 down to 7–4 for the 2005 race, and 12–1 to make it a five-timer in 2006.

This was a great moment for the sport of National Hunt racing and tributes deservedly came pouring in from all quarters. From the trainers' ranks, Jim Dreaper, son of Arkle's trainer, Tom, said, 'I was thrilled to be here to see it. He has equalled Arkle's record in the race now and I would love to see him come back fit and well and try to better it next year.'

Three fingers raised by Jim Culloty in salute to Best Mate's glorious treble at the Cheltenham Gold Cup.

'He is the best horse, that is the long and the short of it. He is good for the game' – legendary Irish owner, J.P. McManus.

'You can't compare horses from different generations but you have to say he is the loveliest and bravest horse. To compare him with Arkle is wrong – that was a different time and a different place – but today was wonderful' – former royal jockey David Mould.

'It was a brilliant performance, especially by the trainer and rider, and he's certainly one of the greatest horses I've ever seen. He showed that he's not just a pretty boy, but that he also has battling qualities' – recently retired jump jockey Norman Williamson.

'He had to fight but character and guts are what the Gold Cup is all about' – politician Robin Cook.

'There is no comparison as Arkle was Arkle and Best Mate is Best

There were lots of hands to be shaken and well-wishers galore, after Best Mate completed his third successive win.

Mate. They are generations apart, but Best Mate is the best three-mile chaser of my era' – trainer Paul Nicholls.

'By toughing it out like he did today, Best Mate has achieved greatness. Whether he is as good as Arkle or not is irrelevant' – former multiple champion jockey Peter Scudamore.

'He's a great horse, it's as simple as that. It's a long time since we saw a horse win a third Gold Cup and it will be a long time before we see one do it again' – Ted Walsh, Irish trainer and former champion amateur.

'Best Mate's win was excellent for racing and excellent for the industry in general. Every sport needs its hero' – Cheltenham's managing director, Edward Gillespie.

The Princess Royal presented the 2004 totesport Cheltenham Gold Cup to triumphant owner Jim Lewis.

'Best Mate is a superstar and every sport needs one. He is our greatest shop window, rather like Dessie, a horse that breaks out of the racing pages into news at large. Add to that his quintessentially British and delightfully quirky trainer and husband and you have a fairytale made in heaven' – Peter McNiele, Cheltenham's marketing manager.

21

LOOKING AHEAD

A week after the Gold Cup, Cheltenham Racecourse announced that it would rename the former Courage enclosure, the Best Mate enclosure from the start of the 2004–05 season. The £3.5 million redevelopment, Cheltenham's enclosure with the least expensive tickets, had been opened for the start of the 2004 Festival, and with its Desert Orchid and Dawn Run Grandstands the capacity increased to 12,500.

Edward Gillespie said, 'Make no mistake, this third Gold Cup win is equivalent for our sport of England winning the World Cup. We no longer have to look back to 1966… Contenders for greatness will in future be compared with Best Mate.'

Jim Lewis was delighted. 'What a truly wonderful tribute,' he said.

Among the letters published in the *Racing Post* after the race was one from Jim Lewis, praising his jockey:

… A jockey's life is difficult and stormy (with apologies to Rodgers & Hammerstein) and my admiration is for the man from Killarney, with a brain as sharp as a razor and a nerve as cool as the deep waters of Lough Leane, who propelled Best Mate into history on Thursday, March 18th, 2004.

We witnessed a poetry and emotion that might have been inspired by the aforementioned composers, but this time the conductor was

Jim Culloty and his baton was Best Mate. Thanks JC, your Mom and Dad are proud of you, and so is the world of jump racing.

Best Mate's achievements have spawned a whole new souvenir industry and so in the summer of 2004 Jim Lewis took out a patent on the horse's name, ensuring that in future any souvenirs can only come with his connections' blessings. At the Festival, fans were able to buy authentic mementos from a stand by the Arkle statue. Proceeds were shared between the Injured Jockeys Fund, the International League for the Protection of Horses and Jim Lewis's nominated charity, The Gentlemen's Night Out.

'Make no mistake, this third Gold Cup win is equivalent for our sport of England winning the World Cup.'

Nine days after the Gold Cup victory, Best Mate made one of his rare public appearances at his local track, Newbury, parading before the first race. A busy Best Mate souvenir shop was on site.

Jim Lewis's seventieth birthday party was held, appropriately, at Cheltenham in June 2004, and Best Mate and Edredon Bleu were both present, along with nearly 200 guests, many from abroad. After dinner in the Gold Cup suite, which was bedecked with claret and blue flowers, representing the owner's famous racing colours, eight speakers, including Henrietta, talked of different times in Jim Lewis's life.

Of his equine stars, Jim Lewis then told the assembled company that the two horses were looking a bit fat. 'They usually start light work – just walking – on 1 July and this year will be no different. They are on course to return in November,' reported Andrew Scutts, in the *Racing Post*.

So, it's on to 2005. Previous protagonists are expected to try again – maybe Beef or Salmon can fulfil early hopes – and new ones, including the highly regarded Kingscliff, may join the fray for the first time,

Beef or Salmon, who could be one of Best Mate's main threats in the Gold Cup of 2005.

as well as graduates from the hurdling field. An intriguing French horse by the name of Kotkijet may be entered. In May he won his second Grand Steeple-Chase de Paris, France's Grand National. To date, the nine-year-old has won fifteen of his twenty-one races, all of them at Auteuil. Healthy competition keeps any sport or business alive and the current king, and his connections, are sure to relish the challenge.

Racing needs the Best Mates of this world. Everyone loves a hero and they come along but rarely, which makes them all the more welcome when they do.

Best Mate is a most appealing horse. He doesn't throw tantrums and he doesn't seem to have off days. He is a regular nice guy, with charm, personality and charisma, what used to be called 'it'. If he were human, he would turn all heads when he entered a room full of people. He would be as happy to talk to the servants as he would to

Kingscliff is another horse who may challenge Best Mate's search for a fourth Gold Cup.

lords and ladies, and he would make everyone feel equally at home. You could almost say he has the 'Queen Mother' touch.

He is lucky to have had just one adoring and appreciative owner and one highly talented, dedicated, skilful and caring trainer, as well as a likeable jockey who deserves every moment of his success.

Whatever the future holds, Best Mate and his connections have done nothing but good for steeplechasing. There is much to look forward to in 2005 when, in an exciting venture, Cheltenham extends the Festival for the first time to a fourth day. Best Mate's date with destiny, his attempt at a fourth Gold Cup, will be on the fourth day, Friday, 18 March – good luck, Matey.

PICTURE CREDITS